WEIGH MORE THAN A PUN A DAY

...PLUS IRONY

SCOTT PATRICK McGOWAN

ISBN-13:

978-1974401253

ISBN-10:

1974401251

THE CREATION OF WEIGH MORE THAN A PUN A DAY

PLUS IRONY

Many people have often told me that I have a way with words — especially in terms of wit. I seem to have a natural knack for creating puns and wordplays, and often surprise others with just how spontaneous my generation can be (despite our collective reputation for being rather regimented). I just seem to have a way of working them into conversations and they usually seem glaringly obvious to me. It is nearly effortless on my end... My verbal antics are more or less simply a part of my basic temperament — a part of my make-up, but much more than cosmetic as it seems to be deeply ingrained in me.

In more recent years, my ability seems to have come into its own....and in keeping with my long-standing musicianship, on what seems to be an even greater scale than ever. In fact, in the last few years prior to initiating this literary project, friends and acquaintances were more frequently asking if I wrote my puns down.

I did, in fact, write some of them down. Many others I had come up with, I simply remembered.

As I continued to share more spontaneously created puns in social gatherings, I began to realize that perhaps my penchant for punning warranted greater formal organization and sharing.

As my propensity for creating puns continued, with the encouragement of my wife and some friends, especially Christian Ty, (a.k.a. "Kidd") I finally decided to write this book.

I began organizing my puns on St. Patrick's Day of 2017 and over a 33 day period created a first rough draft of what is herein contained. Easily more than half of the content of this book consists of newer original material that was sparked in the creative process of organizing what I already had documented in the past (or carried around in my head). I then took a few week break before starting to re-read and edit my material in collaboration with my wife, Harlene.

I then put the project aside, not feeling quite ready to go through the process of securing a publisher who would be willing to open new doors for me by handling my book.

In July of 2017, after some research about how best to proceed, I decided to partner with Amazon's self-publishing platform and on August 16, 2017 received my paperback proof for some final proofing and edits.

Two days later, without warning, the most painful experience of my life occurred when my wife of 23 years, Harlene, with no known heart condition, died at home of a sudden cardiac arrest.

With the support of friends and family, and counselor, Dr. Ari Miller, I have been journeying through a deep dark night of the soul.

At the end of March of 2018, as the emotional storm was beginning to subside and my outlook improving, I picked up my paperback proof and began working on my very final edits, knowing full well that Harlene would never want her passing to cause me to put my uncompleted book on the shelf. During this process, much to my surprise, I discovered that I was even able to elaborate on some of the material due to the apparent reemergence of my adept and playful approach to language. I spent a few hours each day over the next few weekends editing and embellishing, ultimately ending this somewhat unfairly taxing but binding process on April 15th.

I would like to thank my late wife, Harlene for her involvement and support in my first literary creation, including her great patience and dedication in carefully formatting the text as well as the technical aspects of meeting the specs of the Amazon platform for the production of the paperback proof that I used for the very final proof reading and editing.

A heartfelt thanks also goes to Rick Esterson who also provided assistance in this process, with regards to the covers and interior images for the production of the original proof. Thanks also to my dear friend, Phil Woolfson (Maxx Mayhem), as well, who, similarly made the production and availability of the very final version of my book possible by handling those very same technical challenges involved in producing the original proof, including improving the image quality of the dozen or so pictures contained in the interior of the book.

Maxx built upon my original cover designs by improving the image quality of the pictures on the front and back covers and modifying their size and positioning. He also changed the positioning, font choices and font sizes for all of the wording on the covers as well, making for a much more professional and aesthetically pleasing appearance.

Great thanks also to my son Stephen who greatly helped with his computer knowledge and technical assistance along the way.

I would also like to thank my father, Patrick, for sending me to private school and paying for my college education as well as my years of piano lessons. I'm quite certain that those factored greatly into developing my knowledge and skills in the use of language.

I can only imagine how terribly this book would have turned out without Paige Turner, (a(_)muse) who inspired in me a level of literary precision that will hopefully keep every single reader, regardless of their marital status, happily engaged and entertained by the words we put together.

My dearest Harlene, I know that somewhere you are smiling that I have found the strength and determination to return to and complete my first literary project and to go on with my life with your love and blessings. I will keep you deep in my heart forever and fully expect, along with our friends, to strongly sense your presence and spirit in the midst of the book release party on Sunday, May 27, 2018.

My mother, Carol McGowan Circa 1977

My father, Patrick McGowan & father-in-law Irving Davis

Circa 1998

My paternal grandparents "Turk & Geezil" in the 1980s

(Charles & Loretta)

JUST CHILLIN' IN MY HANGING BUBBLE CHAIR IN MY BASEMENT REC ROOM

WITH MY COPYCAT, MONA

I MUST BE TOTALLY OUT OF MY MIND

HERE'S THE FINAL PROOF

"I NEVER INTENDED TO INSPIRE THIS ATROCIOUS TYPE

OF MANSLAUGHTER,

BUT THE APOSTROPHE AND SPACE BAR WERE BROKEN

...AND WERE THE KEY FACTORS IN THIS UNAVOIDABLE

TRAGEDY."

After a series of unfortunate accidents, the transportation industry is finally turning the corner...Apparently the latest intervention is paving the way to much greater safety and is quickly becoming a smashing success.

What is it with this seeming attraction on Facebook between religious women & Type A men? Maybe it's just some specific order, but I will never really be sure unless and until I receive confirmation.

I've always liked a woman who can multi-task, but I did not find it so impressive when Suzie proved to me that she could pick up the phone and get a hold of Howard's johnson.

I know a nudist re-transgender surgeon with a great mental facility who, ironically, barely re-members her patients.

The first Great Pyramid Scheme started with a narcissistic Pharaoh. Ironically, despite his plot to dominate, in the end he wound up (as a mummy) being buried.

I have never joined the mile-high club, BUT I REALLY DON'T GIVE A FLYING FUCK!

However, I know a couple who did it a few times in a row (17) who thought it was really out of sight, but it turned out it was all caught on camera.

My friend tried to talk his girlfriend into it, but after having heard about this couple that was recently caught, she was really up in the air about it.

(credit to my friend Maxx Mayhem for the "up in the air" reference)

Don't you just hate it when you order a draft beer and the barmaid gives you too much head??

...but you live and learn. In fact, a bar is not a bad place to brush up on your language skills. That's where I picked up a lot of sin tax. It's given me a lot of practice in ordering correctly...

I have many wonderful memories of the great times I have spent behind bars.

I just don't know any social norms. It seems like all the Norms I ever meet turn out to be rather introverted. Someone mentioned to me that most social Norms are often well established as a natural result of their extroversion and people skills. I think they are right and perhaps I am simply not following them because I don't NORMally frequent overcrowded high end venues.

If I did, I'm sure I would wind up rubbing elbows with many very well-heeled people. However, being unsure of the laws governing social interactions between the elites, I am concerned that in my old hushpuppies, I might quickly get caught flat-footed.

Besides which, in subjecting myself to the kind of situation that would trigger my claustrophobia, I could easily end up feeling way too close to people that I couldn't even begin to relate to....

Sheila got into a serious disagreement with her hairdresser and stopped using her services. When asked what the problem was she told us that she just would not stop teasing her hair.

Unlike her recent skin graft, this was really no skin off of the hairdresser's back. After all, she only cut hair on the side (which made for a very trendy look). It wasn't like it was her permanent job.

Even so, It certainly was working out better than her former job at the massage parlor where too many customers had complained that she just rubbed them the wrong way...

I know of a local church that uses a criminal background screening software to ensure that the new ministers they hire don't have any convictions. It seems to be working out quite well from a safety standpoint. However, a series of new searches continues as none of them seem to be able to create very inspiring sermons.

As a result, the continuous search has produced quite a collection. Very impressive for a non-denominational church that prefers $100 bills, but their finances are not doing so well.

...People sometimes seek spirituality in other places as well, like one of my neighbors who told me that she once belonged to a nudist commune that held group meditations. As she spoke with me about this, she recounted how one day during a particularly long "om", she had suddenly became disenchanted and ran away, barely escaping...

She, as you might suspect, was quite the idealist. She insisted on "right livelihood" and had initially joined the commune, when she realized that in trying to make it as an artist, she had really painted herself into a corner...

I, myself feel quite fortunate that I've been able to make it in the arts. As a musician, I am really happy that I learned to read music so that I can play popular songs. I'm often asked if I write music myself. Truth be told, I rarely compose myself.

Unless of course, the formality of the occasion absolutely requires it.

Have you ever met a bi polar bear who can't seem to find the right prescription? They're really screwed either way.

I was recently challenged to dominate in a sub mission. The goal was to find a sandwich shop with superior sub standards. I really got on a roll and threw my supporters some red meat when I eventually found the best one. They always deliver.

A friend of mine was traumatized at his own bris, having the misfortune of a mohel who was feeling particularly snippy that day. To either create or save further embarrassment, his family cut the whole thing short. Years later, his medical therapist was astounded when she examined him privately and found it grew some.

Many who contemplate the reason for the sky-high divorce rate do not realize how obvious the answer is. After all, everyone who gets married in a church does so in an excitedly altared state.

The difference between a compliment and an insult is not always so obvious. Like the barfly, Lolli who reportedly gives a really sucky blowjob.

During the Vietnam era, a lot of the Powers That Be found many children that disagreed with them (very) revolting. A conservative friend of mine who happens to be an electrician was never among those who were so reviled by the Establishment. He always refused to revolt.

It is not always easy being the photographer for mugshots. You have to capture them at just the right moment...(but one could always look for another kind of job - one that isn't necessarily so confining.)

Ever since her accident I have been feeling so badly for Lisa. Her car has been fixed, but she's still a total wreck. With all of the days Lisa is missing at work due to these mental health issues, she is on the road to a huge financial crunch.

I've been told that I sure have a lot of sordid / sworded comments for someone who was supposed to have been taught chivalry at a special (k)night school.

The cemetery was auctioning off more lots in a grand plot to keep from going under. No one was sure how things would turn out as they were still awaiting more bid(s).

Jim's jigsaw seemed to be missing...Very puzzling.

When I was a kid, a friend of mine had a dog that could retrieve a stick from more than a mile away.

Maybe that's true...or it might just be another far-fetched story...

Since the crash of 2008, the upholstery shop has never recovered. Among all of the stores along the local strip mall, there is only one that I heard of that is doing surprisingly well these days. You might remember it – the laundry service that folded. At one point, their business had been barely hanging by a thread, but apparently they now have everything ironed out, which is leaving some of the jealous owners of the recently failed businesses nearby steaming mad. Perhaps this has a lot to do with the current setting.

Two podiatrists unknowingly opened up practices in the same office park and soon became arch enemies. The local media learned what was afoot and the situation quickly spawned a reality show, successfully nailing with live footage their increasingly callous attitudes towards each other as they continued to go toe to toe in search of their respective rival's Achilles heel.

Tragically, a cruise ship sank at sea, leaving its once relaxed passengers suddenly and unexpectedly flailing about in the water struggling for their very survival.

In a certain much less pleasant sense they were all still in the same boat...but things were not going so swimmingly...

I know quite a few off-beat musicians who share an exquisite sense of timing. This does not mean they are all the same. In fact, when they get together for group performances, many different values come into play.

The doctor, fearing for his patient insisted that he give up swimming on account of his terrible stroke.

I don't mean to sound redundant, but did I introduce you to my friend from Jamaica? Irie Pete?

As an assertive musician who enjoys puns and Facebook, you must understand that my basic rule states that word plays are fine as per former posts...

When I was in college, several of my classmates pounced on an opportunity to study abroad for a semester, but even after all that time, they still couldn't figure her out.

Miss Taree remained an enigma.

As the plumber was finishing up with one of his few remaining very early bird clients, as his work was drying up, it really began dawning on him. His hopes were really going down the drain...plunging him into a deep depression.

"...and do you, Phil Andering", the priest continued, "take Lucy Strays, forsaking all others?"...

Gun rights are really getting out of control. When a gun won't work, you can't even fire it anymore...

I met a man who practiced bestiality and said that sex with sheep could be sheer ecstasy..."Especially in a see through nightie" he added.

I'm looking to start my own cemetery and am seeking a business partner. Can you dig?

Even in terms of the crematorium, I want to build this business from the ground up. I don't want to just bulldoze everyone. I know how that is because I worked for a cemetery for atheists and was forced to work the most ungodly hours. If you should ever happen upon my old boss, please let him know that I never did find that humerus.

Before that, I worked for a muffler shop. The hours were much more reasonable, but I still found it exhausting.

In taking my driving test, I knew I was good at parallel parking, but didn't give it that much thought. When I was awarded my license, they told me that in that particular area my skills were totally unparalleled.

That was a real turning point in my life.

After a particularly intense high-pitched argument with his girlfriend, the guitarist tuned her out and began to fret that he had wound up with yet another picky, high-strung woman. The progression of this pattern never struck the right chord with him at all.

Perhaps, he thought to himself, being from a whole different social strata cast 'er into a special category that tended to amplify her neurotic tendencies.

I have subscribed to Psychology Today for many years. I have a lot of issues.

In high school I had a teacher who was jealous of my ability to make wordplays. One day he actually began shouting at me after I blurted out a joke. "Scott" he yelled, "your innate ability to pun really pisses me off."

I thought that was a little over the top...

What's your analysis?

I knew a very unattractive woman who was let go from a secretarial job. Constantly keeping her finger on the pulse of the employment market, after a lengthy search for another job, she was finally hired as a cardiologist's assistant. The heart doctor took one look at her and said "I need someone who can really help me to re-pulse my patients. I don't think anyone could beat you in that department. You'll be a natural." Once she was officially hired, no longer disheartened, the doctor retired to his chambers.

Due to a freakish unforeseen accident on the job, a very clean-cut, swishy window washer's career has been shattered. He is looking for a new job now, but has severe limitations. It's very clear to see. It's a real pane in the ass.

The auto mechanic, who didn't strike me as a financial wizard, once again promised me that he really could help me to retire. "You really help people retire?" I asked. "How's that working?" "Very well" he answered. "It's NOT!"

The newly licensed teenager was experiencing a contagious kind of excitement regarding his new car.

...Even the windows were wound up!

When she told him that he was in the doghouse again he nearly hit the roof. He really thought they were slated for some intimate time. And on top of that he had the shingles. Looked like it would be quite a while with(out) a tail between his legs.

I don't mean to get so political here, but I really disagree with Trump's whirled view.

The overly haughty owner of the copy center was proud of his work and often put it on display. Prints of a man!

I know a retired gentleman who became an electrician's apprentice just as a hobby. He said it simply sparked his interest. I guess everyone needs an outlet. I think once I retire I will prefer to just totally unplug.

The rather shaggy carpet installers said they didn't mind me playing my music so loudly. They said they could still concentrate on their work until it was time for their lunch break. Turned out they could really cut a rug, even during their down time.

In addition, they did a terrific job and had great customer service. Management later informed me just how thankful they were that I had gotten involved in making the whole process a real joy by keeping the remnants and with unusual and appreciative gusto, padding them on the back.

They even threw in some cleaning products. They really gave me the red carpet treatment.

The nudist contortionist was so excited to show the audience his next feat (:) that he was barely able to contain himself.

The nude ice dancer was so sad to find herself barely skating by. She had misunderstood the original employment ad and very naively thought she could be doing something artistic and expressive all the while making (an) impressive 8 figures. Turns out to be just the reverse. She really could barely survive on her rinky-dink salary. She knew it was a slippery subject, but she really wanted to speak with her boss to request a raise. She just didn't know how to break the ice and wondered if she should get some support and advice from her friend, Peter Sucker, who was a very diplomatic and likeable gay blade.

Otherwise, she feared she could lose her job and find herself skating on thin ice until her finances began spinning out of control.

Crazy thing about metaphors. When you really like them they turn into similes….

The therapist started wondering if something must be wrong with her. After years of therapy, none of her patients were progressing. Then one day she got rid of the low lying chair her patients sat in and replaced it with a couch which sat up quite a bit higher.

Nearly miraculously, it seemed, her patients' deep-seated problems quickly disappeared. Apparently she had just not been couching her advice correctly.

"God, I really work for pee nuts" said the newly hired receptionist to herself as she began leafing through her new employer's numerous 1,000+ page textbooks on Urology.

Even so, she remained excited about her new job, given the generous salary that she received each time they shelled out her pay.

A lot of Obama's detractors kept insisting that he had broken the law and should be hung.

Someone roped Michelle into sharing what she thought of all of this and she said that he already was...

The guy I was speaking with reminded me of one of the characters from Duck Dynasty. He said that he knew how to make his own beer. I told him I might be interested in learning myself and we struck up a deal.

At first we had difficulty coordinating our schedules, as it seemed something was always brewing for at least one of us, but with sufficient effort we were able to develop the perfect solution. Apparently, this guy with all the fur meant it.

As part of their ongoing training, a new up and coming massage company plans on flying their masseuses to Cancun for a special seminar that will teach them how to give massages south of the border.

This news is proving to be a very touchy subject for a very vocal group of puritanical minded church choir members who are attempting to prevent this trip from occurring, adamantly stating that they are not going to take this lying down.

The authorities are seriously considering permanently ending all American-Asian adoptions. There have been many reports that, unfortunately, the children are just becoming much too disOriented.

My girlfriend and I recently shed all of our preconceived notions and tried nude tennis. We were obviously way out of practice as time after time we barely hit it over the net. It took a lot of balls, as we held a set and continued to court this way.

Mormon fathers are notorious for often failing to educate their sons about the drawbacks of polygamy. Shortly after they take their 3rd wives, these typically rural young grooms soon become keenly aware that their entire farming households have udderly turned into 3 ring circuses.

Genuine fo(u)rthcomings tend to be rare.

Swearing her innocence, the uneducated, but sexually charged defendant was excited to have just learned that she might get off with a hung jury.

Although I really would like to be accepted into the exclusive group, I fear my admission would go before the bored.

The upcoming drag show was sure to be fun. All the guys are being encouraged to take advantage of this opportunity to eat, drink and be Mary.

Technology is now playing a greater role in court rooms. In a recent fraud case, pertinent evidence was admitted to the trial all of which was contained on the cell phone of the plaintiff. The con text completely fit in with the surrounding particulars of the issues at hand.

Kathleen was so proud to be married to such a talented architect. She always admired all of his erections and had built a reputation for pointing them out to her friends.

I can't believe that I missed the new urinals at the bar I frequent. Bad aim I guess. When I shared this joke with another patron she later said that she had taken me too literally and that my whole overarching angle had gone completely over her head. Talk about a bad aim...!?

Not knowing he was being stalked over the internet by a fraud detection agent with cornrows (who was nearly the best in his field) the farmer, hoping to sell his dilapidated farm more easily, was displaying several misleading, carefully cropped pictures of his failing venture.

The farmer could really get locked up in this increasingly hairy, dreadful situation. If he does, he should be used as an example to help deter those who dread locks.

Many thought the nun to be quite the hypocrite, finding it fashionable to criticize others for their bad habits.

The couple sat patiently, awaiting their first much needed appointment at the anxiety clinic. The wait became much longer than expected. Being left alone without attention like this did not appear to worsen their symptoms. It did, however, leave the pair annoyed.

Coming highly recommended to them, the group of friends took a much longer drive than usual to check out this new club, passing several (other) joints along the way. After spending several hours at the new place, they had to agree that this new venue really smoked the competition. They really thought that before too long its ultimate success would surely be in the bag.

The hooker, dejected, decided to change careers. There had to be a better way to pay her bills without getting stiffed all the time.

After such a long day, when the foreman suggested the construction workers stay longer to raise the roof, none of them thought that would be any fun at all. Tough pitch I suppose.

She tired of dating a flute playing cliff hanger. He always left her waiting...Last time he said he got held up at the bank...Barring none, of all the men she had ever dated, he was the hardest to reed / read. Was he serious or was he just giving the story a shot?

As a local hang out, it shouldn't be surprising to learn that the delicatessen has its own little sub culture. In fact, they brought it to the lab, but rather than running tests on it, he simply wagged his tail and ate it.

Does anyone know the latest scoop on the new ice cream shop under investigation? I heard there may have been some financial impropriety. Double-dipping. I guess until they are convicted they feel like they can have their cake and eat it too. At least until they get their (just) desserts.

The geometry teacher, having had no idea he was in such poor shape, left his doctor's appointment wondering if there was really any point. He just felt like when it came to improving his health he just kept going around in circles.

I was thinking about selling one of my big mirrors. I reflected on it for some time and then thought: Oh my God, I better get rid of this thing right away!

The math teacher, despite his innocence, knew his number could still be up when he was accused of spending many years encouraging his students to count less in fractions. His separation was inevitable, but only due to a huge misunderstanding.

They ended up compounding his sentence by refusing to see how he had parsed his words and thereby had contributed to the incarceration of an innocent man.

It's never a good thing to go around with a chip on your shoulder, especially if you're a fugitive. They're tracking more of them down that way these days.

As part of the testimony against the English teacher accused of pedophilia, it was pointed out that he kept several young girls after school on a regular basis, drawing explicit diagrams on the board and telling them exactly where dangling participles are supposed to be inserted. Apparently he didn't know as much about sentences as he should have.

Maybe he should have refrained from drilling them so often?

During his incarceration, he decided that he would change careers and teach biology instead. Certainly by the time of his release he would have learned quite a lot about cells already. He thought this would be the key to escaping further legal problems, rather than becoming an art teacher, who, drawing from his own experience, could easily be perceived as a little too sketchy.

However things work out in the long run, I guess he can just chalk it all up to experience.

The principal, (a former accountant) having too much else to attend to, decided that the new teaching intern should spend the day with the Phys Ed. teacher, Jim Matts. He figured he could keep her on track and show her the ropes.

Despite her lack of athletic ability, they both totally flipped for each other and before too long she was brought on as a Home Ec. Teacher. They developed a healthy relationship in which no one was keeping score so it all panned out well.

There is a real reason for the stench of Sulphur in hell. It all started with a match made in heaven.

Seems I lost all of my inhibitions many years ago. I've been searching for them for quite some time, but so far...no luck.

A decidedly amorous young girl who prided herself on her sense of fashion wore some very tight pants to the club, unsure if she could really pull them off. She brought a guy home with her that night, and as it turned out – she really could.

Such a peel!

An astronaut with free floating anxiety was sent on a mission to the moon. The gravity of his condition caused the mission to crater.

Apparently, when it came to conducting the mental health exam, the supervising team had totally spaced-out. Now that the situation has been remedied, the current applicants for future missions are either (so) completely over the moon and / or could care less.

One night after having a lot to drink, I became so relaxed that my mind began to develop some unusually profound personal insights from a whole different perspective. I meant to write them down, but before too long I lost these alcohol induced epiphanies. -whizzed 'em down the toilet.

The controversy over the Dakota pipeline has fueled a lot of anger according to one unusually energetic underground source. The folks on both sides of the fence keep picketing and perceive their respective political opponents as crude, unrefined and always looking for new ways to be slick.

There is so much talk these days about the epidemic of childhood obesity that it is difficult to digest it all. I am a little concerned myself, feeling like we have lost a very important family value. After all, I always thought that one of parents' greatest objectives was to help their children develop into truly well-rounded young adults.

AS A MUSICAL ARTIST WHO CAN BARELY DRAW

A STICK FIGURE WHILE FULLY DRESSED

I'M TOLD THAT WHEN I SING AND PERFORM MUSIC

I CAN REALLY DRAW A CROWD.

PERHAPS IN JOINING THE CLUB, THAT'S WHEN THE

SHARPEST PENCIL IN THE BOX COMES IN(_)TO PLAY.

Please pardon me for pun-tificating if you will for just a moment, as I wanted to elucidate many of you on questions I have often been asked in regards to my punning prowess. At times, it seems almost like my brain is a virtual pun factory that will never fold. I realize that it can be quite a convoluted (t)issue.

Punning comes as naturally to me as it does when I'm clothed. Just ask my friend with the lisp, who, upon reaching the front door to the nudist colony read the sign he came across out loud "Clothed on casual Fridays."

My friend, Thad Lee returned to my car to share this news.

My mental facility does not shut down, but I don't need a special rubber room like the overstocked condom factory downtown.

Making puns is a sometimes under-rated artful form of humor. In fact, there are punning contests. I am not interested in entering one, but if I did, I'm told I might be in the running due to my cunning and sometimes stunning penchant for punning. However, most likely, I would rather be funning and sunning.

As far as the promotion of my pun factory goes, it's like I'm half-off all of the time, easily sa(i)ling through commercially supported channels that I breeze through with the wind, seemingly, perpetually at my back.

It's almost as if my buoyant personality keeps me in the creative flow of an unusual stream of consciousness that quickly leads to these babbling b(r)ooks which, in getting shipped out keep me afloat.

Perhaps, through the distribution of my published writing, I could literally become a well-known figure of speech via a reputation built through the carefully positioned displays I have in store(s) for everyone.

If none of this bowls you over, or you think my mind's in the gutter, it just might not be up your alley. Maybe you don't have the time to spare, or it just might not, as I mentioned earlier, strike your fancy. It may even push your buttons, while countless scores of others are swept off of their feet.

There's no need to pin the blame on anyone. It's not like anyone was framed.

There's really no contest.

Some people just enjoy wordplays more than others. For those who like to match wits, it can be fun to engage in a verbal back and forth with one or more other people.

I greatly enjoy such banter with my friend, Myles N. Sheath who is a neurologist and a former factory worker with nerves of steel.

I'm so grateful for his friendship. It really was a stroke of good luck that we met. He injects so much humor into nearly every conversation which only seems to needle the more serious types.

I was (a) patient with him during a brief period of time when I was a ladderman. I soon found that he really didn't get on my nerves so much, since a quick examination revealed a clean bill of health. This extinguished any lingering fears (largely produced by a recent conversation with a farmer and former stagehand with hypochondria) that, rather alarmed, I had been entertaining regarding my overall health.

Of course I had to pay. He told me that I couldn't just get off Scott free.

It was my pleasure, and I could not be happier knowing that I introduced him to his wife, and in so doing, helped him unsubscribe to the sexually charged sin apps on his phone.

SECTION 2

I tried on the army gear and became instantly fatigued. I guess I never was cut out for the armed services. Plus, with the ever decreasing benefits they really give you a haircut...I don't think I would like that. I stopped cutting my hair a couple of years ago and like the look of it. It's really been growing on me.

Perceiving himself as a champion of patriotism, the retired military officer spent his entire Veteran's Day flagging posts on social media that he felt were not in keeping with his vision of what it meant to be an American.

The patient who needed life-saving surgery asked the doctor if there were any discounts based on income, but he stated that his fees were non-negotiable and that's just how he operated. The news cut like a knife. The surgeon really had his practice sewn up tight and with the exorbitant medical costs incurred, at many of his patients' requests, he rarely left them in stitches for long, if at all.

I heard that the Erectile Dysfunction clinic was similarly firm on their prices, but at least they occasionally offered sales to the public. This is a relief to many who, unable to afford their standard fees, would never otherwise be able to rise to the occasion. In fact, I came across an e-mail promoting a sale that was being extended for penile enlargements in my junk files. I still can't help but question the potency of their marketing strategy, besides which, when it comes to the performance of the procedure they really squeeze their customers.

The new dance studio owner, having felt cautious about every move, finally opened after much market research feeling like he was two steps ahead of the competition which would enable him to quickly get into the swing of things.

I know of a great new Mexican restaurant with excellent service, but being inclined to hire their own ethnicity, (despite how much this burns up the other job applicants) for the most part, even as they expand their hiring process, they always seem to come up short staffed.

If this ever gets reported to the authorities, they may be forced to allow for (people of) various measures to be employed.

The young musician, feeling quite frustrated and like something was lacking in his first recording, was approached by one of the engineers who gave him some sound advice.

Knowing that the young artist's budget was limited, he let him know where he could get a hummer for a song. In the end, the musician felt that his piece was truly served by this well received suggestion.

Paying careful attention to the importance of hygiene, the hopeful job applicant suddenly realized it might not have been the best idea to be all washed up before his interview. He sure hoped he could find gainful employment soon as he was growing tired of having to sponge off of his family.

His family, in turn, was growing tired of his awful singing in the shower each morning before each of a series of interviews that were, in each instance, temporarily garnering his enthusiasm.

Between this continuous morning routine, his unsuccessful efforts and the drama that kept unfolding, his life was truly turning into a soap opera.

Elizabeth felt very heartened that the young attractive tutor had helped her struggling teenage son improve his academics. At first she was understandably concerned about having her help him bone up on his studies, especially when she had to run to the store and, in taking much longer than expected, having forgotten her cellphone, grew increasingly concerned about a bun in the oven.

With his future in being admitted to a good university hanging in the balance, she wondered to herself just how far he might get.

It was not too much later that the news of his A in Anatomy along with Bertha's positive pregnancy test results confirmed her deepest fears.

She had apparently not been wrong at all in suspecting that something may have been up.

"I still don't quite understand" said the young daring teenage driver to the policeman who had just pulled him over.

"I thought you liked donuts" he said, with sardonic enthusiasm. "Should I sprinkle in some other stunts?" he added. He really was pushing things too far and needed to wake up and smell the coffee, stop stirring things up and just give it a rest before he winds up in trouble.

Trans-plant surgeons are getting a lot more work out in their fields.

Apparently the gender identity issue does (not) vegetate, and now extends to other forms of life as well.

The patient felt eternally grateful to the dentist for having mercy on her financial situation and filling all of her cavities for free (pro-bono). They soon began dating and eventually married.

To this day, he still performs such favors, though technically, with the expansion of his practice and the many credit cards this has afforded them, he wishes she wasn't so much looser than she used to be.

The rich land-owner, self-absorbed in crediting himself for being magnanimous in taking his indentured servant to the beach, never bothered to find out that he could not swim beforehand, and inevitably left his serf bored.

A growing list of similar incidents are creating fertile ground for an insurrection that will be likely to take him by surprise and cause him to soil himself.

The young, uninhibited, horny student, Randy Cooke, attended culinary school only briefly, but growing restless and unsure of his future plans, left his consideration of a career as a scantily clad restaurant chef on the back-burner.

Knowing of the landscaper in question's chemical-dependence issues as well as his tendency toward OCD behavior, when I received news that he had just turned over a new leaf...

I wasn't sure whether to be happy for him or somewhat concerned about the future security of his current career.

I really hope he is out of the woods for good.

Two young musicians, only recently recruited as replacements for a successful rock and roll band sat nervously in the waiting room as the founding members were attending a closed door meeting with a top executive record producer. Finally one turned to the other and said "are you thinking what I'm thinking?" Dejectedly, the other said, "I think so. I really DO have a feeling we're not in Kansas anymore"...

"Well just in case" said the first one, "I heard of another opportunity. Maybe we can join Toto."

...or maybe they could form their own band and build upon their current repertoire.

As they discussed this they discovered they both knew a bunch of completely random, unrelated classic rock songs.

Among them: Witchy Woman, Red Shoes (Facedancer), Tin Man, I Had Too Much to Dream Last Night (The Electric Prunes), I Put a Spell on You, Goodbye Yellow Brick Road, Scarecrow (Dan Fogelberg), The Wizard (Black Sabbath), Crystal Ball (Styx) & Can't Find My Way Home.

Despite increasingly polarized points of view, both sides agreed that Trump really was promising everyone a golden shower.

Finally... a connecting point to help heal the deep divide in the country. Seems like people are really pissed.

Maybe not so coincidentally, as my music school expands, I seem to be gaining more in tuition.

Speaking of intuition, I know of a freelance psychic whose practice is the center of much debate.

She has made a great number of accurate predictions, but tends to be scattered and does not focus on her bookkeeping very well.

As such whenever anyone claims that she is right on the money, the arguments inevitably ensue.

It's easy to guess which side of the fence General Ledger is on regarding all of this. The semi-retired drill sergeant turned accountant, examined her overall abilities and stated for the record, that unlike his regimented practices, her left and right columns were not even, nor were all of the required figures present and accounted for...

Connor's mother took him to the children's Ninja Turtles event, hoping that exposing him to his very favorite superheroes might help him overcome his painful shyness.

She really enjoyed the improved aesthetics as well, seeing that the rep tiled the floor exactly as he had previously described as being in the planning stages at the time she purchased the tickets in advance.

Given the opportunity to receive an autographed book from Donatello, she smiled with relief when she saw signs that he was finally coming out of his shell.

Brandy really was a fine girl, and was pleasantly surprised to one day meet a sailor who wound up (he was very excited) tying the knot with her.

She was so excited to be married, as she and her friends had really thought that ship had sailed, but apparently the tide had turned.

I wanted to start a unique new enterprise with a novel concept: a bookstore with a full-menu restaurant.

I was deeply disappointed when I found out the unaffordable cost of meeting the necessary requirements of the bureaucrat from the health department. He insisted that due to the very close proximity between the murder mystery book section and the area where food would be served that there would have to be regular inspections for bookworms.

So, in search of other ideas, I thought of opening a men's footwear store, but then thought, starting on a shoestring would make the whole store I was envisioning so laced with problems that it would tie my stomach in knots, causing me to engage in some serious sole /soul-searching.

In speaking with others about my aspirations, some gave me quite a tongue lashing, but a few others referred me to the previously referenced psychic who was reportedly a terrible bookkeeper, but a shoe-in for an accurate reading.

She asked me to bring in a high-top to connect with its energy, as a sort of mini-oracle. She told me that she saw an unexpected windfall coming my way shortly, and told me not to lose hope.

Now that a year has gone by, I can tell you unabashedly, that the Converse was true.

I know an ethically challenged, music-loving, overweight police officer with a terrible sense of rhythm who always seems to be on the beat. Bi and large,(XXXL) (t)his bad Dan Singh suffers greatly due to a rare genetic disorder, which caused him to be born with two left feet. From what I understand, despite this, with potential opportunities for sadistically pleasurable contact with both men and women alike, he really enjoys his clubs and hits them whenever he can.

I don't mean to insert myself here, but your laptop screen says that you need to include one special character in setting up your new password and I thought maybe I could help...

Typically, reciprocity is appreciated. However, when the home improvement representative worked so diligently to ensure that his clients' counter fit he did not feel particularly amused when the bills they paid him with turned out to be counterfeit.

Every time my ex communicates I feel completely alienated and like I am going to hell. Almost like I committed some kind of unforgivable crime and am being preached to by someone who has the power to subject me to some kind of eternal damnation. God she really burns me up.

Please pardon the submission of this letter, but as you will see, it explains exactly why I am absolutely refusing to cooperate with the pointless requests and edicts to which your board is attempting to force my compliance.

The free spirited employee of the dance studio came waltzing in late again with the same old song and dance regarding her astrological chart and how Leo tardiness is a common trait with many people of her zodiac sign.

In couples with varying libidos it remains important that they learn to compromise regarding the frequency of sexual intercourse.

Unless there is an issue with complete abstinence, couples usually find a way to eventually meet in the middle.

A lot of Trump supporters thought he was going to really shake things up inside the beltway and take the Capitol by storm. Oddly enough, his base was actually quite happy when he refused to tour NATO.

Company management and the recently dismissed worker had different points of view regarding the issue of him falling down on the job.

The worker had filed a wrongful termination suit as well as a workers' comp case regarding an alleged accident and injury on the job.

During testimony, management agreed that he fell down on the job, but said that it was repeatedly and had nothing to do with a slippery floor.

I know an unhandicapped attorney, Peg Legg, who absolutely refuses to represent paraplegics swearing she could never build a strong case for clients without a leg to stand on.

It was part of the routine for customers to have shorter waits for punchlines at the comedy club's shows than at their after-hours parties.

Apparently, the refreshments served at these exclusive post-show gatherings were spiked.

In keeping with the elevated spirits that the seemingly perpetual toasts that were so super, naturally inspired, they continued to really pour it out.

These parties, nearly without fail, end up spilling out until the wee hours of the morning.

I once heard it said that during election years, analysis has showed that the polls go up whenever the voters get excited.

It was a once in a lifetime experience to have our doorbell ring and to answer the door only to discover that it was a set of Siamese twin girl scouts trying to sell us Tagalongs.

Months later, I happened to bump into them at the local grocery store along with their mother.

I got to talking to her and nodded in agreement as she continued describing how close her daughters were and that they truly seemed to be joined at the hip.

In & out of the spirit of the season, on Christmas Day, I grew impatient waiting for the set-up instructions for my new device to download on the internet.

Nearly completely losing all faith, I impatiently shouted "Oh come, oh come E-manual!"

"Why that's as easy as Pi!" exclaimed the math genius with the full figure.

She must have kept a lot of food at home because I can attest to the fact that throughout the semester, including with this particularly long-winded answer, she never went out to lunch even one single time.

Ironically, after meeting a man with severe anxiety and trying to help him to relax by giving that cat a tonic, he suddenly became frozen with fear and downright paranoid.

A local restaurant was shut down due to the health department being notified about a problem with mice.

Given time to rectify the problem, a follow up inspection was conducted by the big cheese (who secretly felt really trapped in his job) and the report came back squeaky clean.

A recent study showed significant reductions in stress levels for those who do Zen a dozen or more times per month.

I once participated in a sleep study. It really was a dream job that paid quite well. I was really making money in my sleep. My boss actually insisted that I lay down on the job, drawing into serious question, at least for me, the old adage "when you snooze you lose."

Through his interaction with and healing of the lepers, Jesus Christ formed a very deep bond with those whom he cured. In the Biblical story, Jesus felt quite despondent that only 1 of the 10 came back to him again, but believe me, when this happened, he smiled soulfully and exuberantly shouted "give me some skin, brother!"

She always kept her sergeant at arms(') length a secret, but judging from her reactions to questions regarding his endowment, there must be more intimacy between them than she is letting on given that she always complains about her financial situation.

A friend of mine has been in an on-again / off again relationship and feels he is ready to move on and find another girlfriend. He said he was looking for a woman with bigger boobs and more money. We wondered if he could successfully connect with the right woman by placing a personal ad for a rich woman with Double D's so that he could milk her for all that she's worth.

Well, the ad finally may have worked. He had a nice conversation with a potential date that fit this description, and more importantly, made her explicitly aware of his sexual penchant for breast humping. "So do you want to go out?" she asked after a while. "Sure", he said, but keep in mind what I told you about my favorite sexual practice" He paused and then said "Just remember. Balls in your quart."

To summer eyes:

Not much else can be seen by many of our youth during those warm months when school is out of session, other than free time, pools and beaches and time for parties and get-togethers.

Before the allegations of sexual misconduct came out, not many people had ever described Donald Trump as the touchy-feely type.

Not all experts agree about how good of exercise various forms of dance are, but at least it's a step in the right direction.

Steve's recent social isolation had seemingly cast a dry spell on his sex life, but then he began taking dance lessons at a local studio and before he knew it, having been taught to swing both ways, his chances for a date on the weekend automatically doubled.

I really have no idea why, but often, when I open up my guitar case I find several dollar bills under my G-string.

When I purchased my guitar, I also bought several accessories including an upright stand for it. Before I even learned to play a single note I had myself a standing Ovation.

When I was 27, having no musical facility whatsoever, I decided to pursue a career providing piano & keyboard lessons in students' homes.

To this day, it is the key component to my livelihood, despite still having no musical facility whatsoever, along with the staff I employ.

Many years back I had a few professional assessments of a seemingly permanent spring in my step(pe).

The psychiatrist, geologist and architect all agreed that although this was unusual, it was relatively harmless.

One of the most serious people I have ever met in my life was a hearing impaired accountant named Joe King.

I attempted to get him to lighten up and get his goat a number of times, but there was just no kidding him allowed / aloud. His wife, So, told me that he felt that refraining from joking helped to keep him out of hot water. Humor just did not figure into his life.

My next door neighbor and I seem to have a growing mutual animosity towards one another. I knew it would not be long before I would have to either completely block my view of his house or take some kind of course in self-defense or physical combat.

In the end I decided to take up fencing.

Recently my friend Rick and I happened upon the fact that both of our aunts had previously worked for Uber and had both had their services terminated by the company under what they each felt were grounds for wrongful termination lawsuits.

Upon further discussion we discovered that both of our aunts were positively livid.

In essence what we had together was a case of totally furious ex-Uber aunts.

Speaking of mood states, as a democratic Marylander with a chronically upbeat personality, I am happy and proud to report that I have perpetually lived in a truly blue state for my entire life.

I know a kid who, apparently not so coincidentally, lost his virginity during a period of time that his academics were absolutely abysmal. The girl who was interested in bedding him took one look at his atrocious report card and exclaimed: "Oh my God, I totally love slow pokes!"

I know this is a most unusual situation, but I know a woman who had an affair with a ghost who swore that the sex was totally out of this world. "Totally unreal!" she (ex)claimed. She became involved in this transdimensional romance when a liberal-minded medium introduced them thinking the world should really give the pair a normal chance.

She got so wrapped up in their relationship that she often forgot that they "came" from different worlds. Finding the whole experience quite intoxicating himself, one night he scared up a little extra cash and met up with his buddies to celebrate in a hauntingly familiar club in a small ghost town and announced to them (loudly, over the din of "Spooky" playing in the background) that he was going to ask her to marry him.

He flew home a few hours later that particularly windy night, planning on proposing to her. He felt a little uncertain what her answer would be. As he neared home he saw her and nervously yelled "will you marry me?"

In suddenly remembering he was a ghost she, quite frightenedly, and starting to look a little ghostly herself answered "yes, but oh my God, you're three sheets to the wind!"

Tragically, and perhaps, not so coincidentally, and in a seemingly significant symbolic occurrence, he wound up being totally blown away at the exact moment of her surprising answer.

Hell bent on financial success, a young entrepreneur, having left his dental practice and feeling like he was really "in the zone" wanted to open a store with a new and unusual angle that he really believed would eventually do well by degrees.

Unfortunately, he ran into problems and could never get the store off the ground when a particularly unpopular, but well known, decidedly unhip zoning bureaucrat (a former hardware store owner) provided some concrete evidence regarding how the store would need to be positioned in relation to the sidewalk. He was very thorough in performing his job which he took quite seriously, and had absolutely no tolerance for cutting corners.

The former dentist and hardware store owner ended up in a heated conflict to the right side of the public square. Knowing that it would be impossible for both of them to have the market cornered in the way that they each wanted, they began fighting...tooth and nail.

In the scuffle, the bureaucrat fell to the ground and wound up so badly injured that as public sentiment grew during his hospitalization, it became increasingly obvious that both he and the department desperately needed a hip replacement.

An undecided busy professional voter had little time to become immersed in the political news during the recent presidential campaigns. As Election Day approached, he became increasingly aware of the great need for a movement.

As he sat on the toilet, he did some googling just to get some bottom line information on just what these ass-wipes were all about. He was truly hungry for information and thought it was a lot to digest during such a brief period for both he and his wife, but found the intestinal fortitude necessary to make for a solid decision with little time to waste.

Feeling great compassion towards the disenfranchised who, often in desperation, needed to pinch a loaf here and there, he chose his candidate through a process of elimination.

As her obesity problem grew, Pearl became less and less well-rounded and many aspects of her life began to suffer. Even her relationship with her race car driving husband, which used to be a gas, began to deteriorate as they grew increasingly tired of the conflicts.

With all of the screaming matches going on as a result of neglect as she no longer lit his fire, the neighbors began to suspect that something was not running smoothly in the hood.

Especially when he came home totally smashed and exhausted one night and yelled at her that she no longer got his motor running. He really blew a gasket and criticized nearly everything about her appearance, stating that even her hair pin turns him off.

He reminded Pearl that her refusal to get on the fast track to recovery was a non-starter for him. He emphasized that the brochures certainly gave more than enough details and she should really tread on it.

As the weeks went by with no rim jobs, the nuts and bolts of their relationship completely corroded. Finally he filed the divorce papers and that's when her world came crashing down around her.

Pearl was so devastated that it was really eating her up inside. When the neighbors saw her next, being the motor mouths that they were, they gossiped that the whale, as they had been calling her, had been blubbering all day so the shit must have really hit the fan.

At least if they couldn't jump-start their relationship with some kind of new spark, they parted ways when it became increasingly obvious that their marriage was really running on fumes.

Pearl told the neighbors she would not be receiving any financial support from him and that she would have to tighten her belt. She made it a key point that otherwise she could end up on skid row, which would really be a total drag.

At this point, no new transmissions have been reported.

After another fire and brimstone sermon near the shoe repair shop, the preacher stopped in and was approached by a salesperson who jokingly asked if he had come in to save his own soul. The preacher, who took his mission very seriously, retorted, "it is quite ungodly to mock a sin."

A young newly hired lifeguard was refusing to conduct the chemical tests on the water as often as his boss insisted. His boss became increasingly annoyed by what he perceived as his new employee's failure to understand the safety standards he had explicitly shared with him.

As time passed, this defiant lifeguard, apparently lacking a filter, continued to skip many of the scheduled times for these tests according to several concerned whistle-blowers.

It proved entirely too difficult for the boss to impress upon this young man his obligation to follow this schedule if he wished to remain employed there, so ultimately he had to skim through the most recently completed job applications to see who might be on deck.

Ultimately, he really had no choice but to fire the young man for testing the waters too much.

The aquarium store had been hitting some rough waters and the owner, especially, felt stuck between a rock and a hard place. Too many customers had waved goodbye lately.

The owner hired a business consultant who gave him a lot of food for thought and pointed out the many areas in which he had been flaking out.

He wanted serious advice and knew better than to take these experts' suggestions with a grain of salt.

After just one session the business owner was totally hooked. He took a poll / pole of his employees too when he had them on the line and they too, agreed that the bait and switch tactics with their customers needed to end.

The issue opened a whole new can of worms, but this unexpected opening helped to anchor them in a whole new, as of yet unexplored depth and they were forever grateful to the consulting school. They really had class. There was nothing fishy at all about their method of reeling in new clients whose businesses were close to hitting rock bottom.

In the end, the aquarium store owner and employees implemented all of the recommendations after having absorbed the most essential information like sponges.

At first, the changes moved things forward at a snail's pace, but as they cut their teeth on the once buried treasures they had received, they were in for smooth sa(i)ling.

Before too long, these new practices became second nature as they filtered down into their day to day operations.

They soon took the town by storm as demand for their products continued to bubble up more and more.

Stocking up on supplies so that they had a lot in (the) store for their growing customer base, the crew continued to steer themselves towards profits that were on a grander scale than they had ever dreamed possible - like nobody's business – so now they're tanking like crazy.

A proctologist who subbed for the local county public school system filled in for an English grammar teacher that many considered to be an asshole.

He was demonstrating the proper use of a colon to the class, and as he became more excited about punctuation marks, the semi-colon.

The students were quite enthusiastic as well as precocious, and after these quick lessons, in a slightly cheeky manner, asked several very good probing questions.

There was one more thing he had meant to explore as well, but at the moment, with the principal ready to conduct the white glove inspection, he grew increasingly nervous, being unable to put his finger on it.

It has been a great pleasure to see the very skilled and talented young carpenter's apprentice, Woody, build his self-confidence during the process of completing several consecutive projects while he continues to progress from his treatments at the local erectile dysfunction clinic.

I still can remember how he used to lumber through the day, totally bored, quite despondent that he hadn't nailed anything.

After years of sobriety, early on in his apprenticeship, he had been tempted to go out and get hammered on screwdrivers, but being level-headed, he was able to take careful measures that helped him to resist.

Now he simply beams with pride, marveling at his own erections.

I am very happy for my friend and his new relationship with a waitress who is a Math Major at the local university.

I hope she never desserts him, except with her pi(e) and certainly never on a Sunda(e)(y).

When he first met her, he was attracted to her, but felt her service was not so good. He was not sure if he was going to put the tip in, but eventually, with her cooperation in fact, he gave her the shaft.

At first, the warden had approved the Erectile Dysfunction clinician's request to hold an information meeting for the prisoners, but now he was having second thoughts feeling it might be irresponsible, given the rehabilitative slant of this facility.

After all, should he really be playing any role in helping to create a bunch of hardened criminals?

With a little more thought, the warden found the balls to make a firm decision against allowing the meeting and reached for the phone wondering how best to soften the blow without coming across too stiffly.

You are cordially invited to our Semi-Annual Pot Lucky Orgy.

We welcome folks of all sexual persuasions so feel free to swing bi and it will be our pleasure to meat you.

Please bring a dish to share.

Musical get-togethers can be quite fun and memorable. It's a great way to escape for a while and forget about any of the troubles and challenges you may face in your day to day life.

After all, who doesn't like to find themselves in a great jam?

Due to transportation issues, the young couple has to deal with sour grapes now that they can't elope. At least that's what I heard through the grapevine. Apparently now they're raisin(') Cain.

If you ever move to Texas, if things start to go south you can always move to the Panhandle.

The mental health facility has strict rules regarding quiet in the lobby area. They never want their patients to be disturbed or to think that they might be hearing voices again.

The musical director of the upcoming production liked to experiment with less strict timing with many of the pieces. This particular show included a piece entitled "Ships" which was one of his favorites of the 20 songs this new musical play was to boast.

Rehearsals were almost complete and the timing was good as this was the last song that the cast had left to master. After going through "Ships" with strict timing, the director, needing a short break from their singing, put on a recording of the song, then requested "now loose lip-synch 'Ships'."

They soon came to know the entire score even more so when, after opening night, many of the show-goers being unusually unimpressed with the lack of strict timing in "Ships" gossiped to the point that the rest of the scheduled shows were canceled due to nearly non-existent ticket sales and the production was deemed a failure.

Dawn could not wait to have a baby and start a family with her new husband, Bubba. She loved him dearly, but never did understand nor approve of his enthusiasm for guns.

They really were a lovely couple and both worked hard at low-level jobs due to their lack of education. Bubba liked to go out in the woods behind their home just before sunrise with his rifle in hopes of improving his hunting skills.

Unbeknownst to him, Dawn was secretly removing his bullets.

When this finally dawned on him, the smoking gun seemed evidence enough and triggered the subsequent dramatic decrease in their intimacy, due to the (paradoxically) increased friction between them, dashing her hopes for pregnancy.

Dawn was completely against him taking pleasure in any kinds of magazines at all. This was not only obvious because of the times she had removed his bullets, but also from the manner in which she had come barreling into the house after having seen him walking the dog out in the yard with an issue of Playboy in his other hand.

The stress of the whole situation was also apparently decreasing his sperm count and before they knew it, it took the help of a counselor, a sex education specialist as well as a fertility clinic to help them realize that their best hope for a future family was for Bubba to stop shooting blanks at the crack of Dawn.

Years later, things were going well for Dawn and Bubba and they were happily and proudly raising three lovely children.

They worked hard to further their education as well. In fact, Bubba had grown quite articulate and had written a novel and was in the process of having it published.

He was disappointed when technical issues arose during the first print run. In his overwhelming excitement, despite this setback, he quickly overcame the issue (quite a contrast to his previous sexual problems) and for the second time, learned yet another lesson in reproduction.

You never hear much about presidents' pets after they leave the White House and the next president is sworn in. I only recently became aware, given this, that Bill Clinton has two new very fetching dogs named Neil and Bob.

I recently found the perfect place for a picnic in a no-fly zone.

The unusually hip, part-time bricklayers in the old small town village square became annoyed when they discovered that, due to its inconvenient position in relation to the project at hand, they would be forced to work around the clock.

It was difficult for them to adjust to these previously unfamiliar work conditions, but they did over time.

Many of them found it quite odd that earlier on, when they were the most upset about the increased workload, that management, well known for encouraging their workers to suppress the outward expression of any intense emotions, was actually demanding that they punch the clock even more than ever...

My friend and colleague Joel had worked with me at the men's clothing outlet for years. He was one of my best friends and was the kind of guy who would give you the shirt off his back. He was being considered for partner by the owner because of his huge and consistent success in the footwear department. It seemed none could follow in his footsteps. Despite his freakishly tiny feet, he really had big shoes to fill. There was only one other employee, Richard, being considered as well who was a close match in sales ability.

The owner could not decide, so in response he created a sales contest for the upcoming month as the tie-breaker.

Joel rolled up his sleeves and went toe to toe with his competitor, but ultimately, Joel was victorious.

I knew he was a shoe-in compared to this overly buttoned down Dick, and, being annoyed with his abrasive attitude, Joel told him to just put a sock in it. I am so happy for Joel. I feel like this position was really made for him, and as they say, if the shoe fits, wear it.

We are all extraordinary, living breathing miracles. Although we never give it much thought, each and every time we make a fresh post on social media, no matter how seemingly mundane it may feel to us, it truly is, each and every time, at least for a brief instant, a post the "likes" of which have never been seen in the history of mankind.

The young man felt so nervous, but was finally ready to "come out" to his father as gay. He finally just uttered the words "Dad, I'm gay" and much to his relief, his father said "no worries son. I've always known anyway, although I never brought it up. Nothing to feel bad about. After all, a sucker is born every day."

There seems to be a real cultural lag in perception regarding head-hunting cannibals and the modern world. Despite their savage appearance and the lack of a suit and tie, business meetings and cellphones, the truth of the matter is even head hunters are just trying to get a head.

They really are quite driven. In fact, most major corporations employ at least one if not several.

There is widespread agreement that one of the surest tell-tale signs of a successful head hunter from either world, is when you can see that they have a good head on their shoulders.

I never quite saw eye to eye with my optometrist and former baseball star, Iris.

Making note of this, she scheduled a corrective surgery and though it was effective, we developed the same problem once again when I received her bill.

I lashed out at her, but being an accomplished pupil of a great and visionary Zen master, without even batting an eye, she calmly explained that she always had to make sure she covered all of her bases in running her practice.

Although she was quite nice, the young lady at the fabric store seemed to not be a very sophisticated person. We made some small talk and after a little while she mentioned how convenient it was working there given all of the materials they sold that she used in her creative projects.

She really felt it was the perfect place for her. So, as it turned out, contrary to my initial impression, which obviously was prefabricated, she really was quite crafty.

Imagine my surprise when I saw my favorite famous anchor person on the same ship as me.

The anorexia support group meetings seem to be growing, while the obesity support groups, on the contrary, seem to be thinning out. The giant meetings have been shrinking and the midget meeting are reaching new heights.

The entire body of the organization will soon be hosting a mixer dance and is hoping to solicit claustrophobics and those suffering from social anxiety as well as motivationally challenged layabouts to come join them for this social event with a mailer that would connect with a message of empathy about knowing what it's like to not want to stand out in a crowd.

In this day and age, it is important for trans parents to have a support group. Especially as they, now like gays and lesbians, want to feel free to "come out". They, too want to know just how good it feels to be transparent.

We know trans parents, see, and would like to use some of them to help project supportive images on the wall that everyone will be able to relate to during the meetings that are soon to take some kind of form. We are open to whatever that may be.

Rumor has it that Putin may have basically said "you're a nation", then pissed all over the U.S., undermining our election and our democracy.

Many of us were concerned about the trampoline artist who had endured some very difficult set-backs on her very last spring semester in college when she was carrying a very heavy load, but with the support of a social safety net, she seems to have bounced right back.

We met a real cowboy at karaoke who told us we probably wouldn't see him for a few weeks as there was so much that he needed to attend to at home.

When he returned a few weeks later we were pleased to see him again and couldn't help but notice how much better his singing was since we had last seen him.

I suppose that happens when you finally give enough attention to improving your range.

A friend of mine was always reluctant to see a new movie without reading plenty of reviews and finding out how the cast rated.

I found the whole process almost too painful to watch. "Come on" I muttered impatiently. "Chop, chop!"

Although I've never been, I heard that things are really hopping down there in Australia.

I recently heard about two albinos, each of whom were married to other people, who were apparently having a dull affair.

Everyone misplaces their keys sometimes. It's such a frustrating experience, especially when you've searched everywhere with no luck at all. I'm sure many of you can recall such fruitless missions that, ironically, rendered you nuts.

Me and my pet agree: mutts are seriously underrated.

Others have various opinions. It really seems, like with any debate, the controversy breeds some pretty mixed results.

Have you ever met someone who is well-off and…..well……"OFF?"

Peter could not believe that the woman of his dreams was marrying another man. He sneaked into the church as the ceremony was getting ready to begin. The minister's words cut him like a knife: "speak now or forever hold your peace."

As the tears filled his eyes, he followed the advice he had obviously misunderstood and without saying a word, reached down into his pants ever so surreptitiously, feeling like he really would never ever let go…

Peter was startled a few moments later when someone else in attendance who overheard his sobs and was obviously annoyed whispered "Please get a hold of yourself."

EVEN MORE SPEICALIZED TRANSMISSIONS FROM THE HEMISPHERES

TOTALLY MENTAL MUSINGS FROM A DECIDEDLY MECHANICALLY CHALLENGED CUNNING LINGUIST

THOSE REPUNS'LL HAVE YOU TEARING YOUR HAIR OUT UNTIL YOU WONT HAVE IT MUCH LONGER

It has been a joy to give birth to this, the third section of my publication.

I have been told by many that I have quite a fertile mind, but I really had no conception until I began to organize my thoughts and scribblings into publication form.

I am grateful that you have taken the time and the interest to now be holding this book in your hands – or viewing it on your handy device.

I truly believe that we have all been put on this Earth for various purposes and much of what is herein contained as well as future publications of mine were and are meant and intended to be shared and put forth on this particular plane of existence for whatever joy or insight they may bring to others.

Life certainly has its share of pains and challenges and humor and whatever cleverly disguised wisdom it may contain can serve as one of those shining lights to help guide us through our most troubling dark nights of the soul.

Should one of life's inevitable and difficult transitions or enduring stressful circumstances be engulfing you at this particular moment in time, it is my sincere hope that you find some comfort and respite in reading my writing which I believe Spirit has compelled and inspired me to create and share.

SECTION 3

Matt found the new computer program a bit challenging. When he spoke to management about it, having been such a great employee for so many years, they created a new format for Matt and before too long it all began to click for him.

I once had an affair with an elevator operator. I had really thought that together, we had taken our relationship to a whole new level, but she complained that I really just pushed all of her buttons. In, retrospect, I should have known that she'd take me for a ride.

Not much later, after the break-up, I had a whirlwind affair with a weather reporter, Windy, whom I felt really had quite a sunny disposition. Getting along with her was a breeze.

Some others perceived her personality quite differently, however, and said she was stuck-up and put on cold airs, but whether vain or not, with the exception of one particularly windy night when a sensitive issue seemed to precipitate an argument that seemed to go round and round before we finally cleared the air, I can currently report that our relationship is far from stormy and that things really seem to be pointing in a whole new direction.

Even her friends, who are far from fair-weather friends and never put on a front, are now chiming in that their previous doubts were just cloudy perceptions that seem to be evaporating, especially once they caught wind that many of their acquaintances who always seem to know which way the wind is blowing truly believe that our relationship will soon begin taking the town by storm.

Shannon loved the band that was playing at the local club where she was bartending on Halloween night, but to her dismay, being short staffed and with so many people ordering bottled beer, she spent her entire shift twisting the night away.

About 5 years ago as I began to reach a bottleneck in my weight loss efforts, I came to the somewhat sobering conclusion that the real skinny on the issue was that I would have to cut down on the number of nights I drank beer if I expected my efforts to continue to pay off.

It was easy and did not matter much to me. I'm still a happy camper who happens to prefer tropical beaches.

I really seem to stay in good spirits, even when good spirits are not in me.

But when the going gets a little rough (or not) I still think beer is a great solution.

Taking stock of the importance of appearance during business meetings, I dressed neatly and appropriately to connect with my potential future business partner at the restaurant where he was currently the sole owner. Good thing I could get there safely, having had a tire change the day before. So I found my way there knowing it was right to go in vest.

We reached an agreement and my new business partner mentioned that he could tell simply by my otherwise unwarranted pants (the fashion police were never contacted) just how excited I was about the opportunity.

They say it is a compliment to personalize gifts to match the personality of the receiver so I gave some gifts to some close friends that didn't seem to be wrapped too tight.

I cannot believe I misplaced my pen again. I do not have the slightest inkling where I put it.

If you don't have virgin eyes and are of proper age could you please grab the magnifying glass and help me find where my pen is.

Sorry, but I am just feeling very disconnected right now.

When it comes to the execution of terrible legislation, I am completely in favor of killing the Bill.

A very sketchy art student who walks dogs on the side and has a Spotless record recently took up with an extremely straight-laced sewing instructor who is as cute as a button and keeping him in stitches.

Their relationship has been drawing the ire of many who feel like they are a poor match and are barking up the wrong tree.

The truth of the matter is there are many wonderful aspects of their relationship that most people aren't aware of that, when taken into consideration, rather than using such a broad-brush, paint an entirely different picture.

There is one particularly painful lesson to be learned by men considering receiving oral sex from imaginary creatures: Dragon teeth.

Sharonda really hated the rather gross(ly) underpaid Caucasian urologist for whom she worked. At lunch time in the cafeteria, that white bread pee nut butt her way through the line and sandwiched herself between a good friend of hers and another woman who also hated her; an extremely short woman with a "rye" sense of humor who loved music jams with whom she never seemed to quite see eye to eye.

I actually have participated in a few of her jams. Even refreshments are served and she offers quite a spread. They're really quite peachy, and though I'm a little fuzzy, I seem to recall that she preserves an amicable atmosphere by not allowing people with such piss-poor attitudes to join in.

The freelance pet sitter had given up her blue collar job to walk a different path.

As her services began to fetch greater and greater profits, her parents couldn't have been happier for her that she had finally unleashed her true potential.

They were so proud of her that they posted a picture of her on Facebook in which they even tagged one of her favorite dogs.

With few signs of intelligent life at home, the astronaut, (a Moonie who had ironically never bared his buttocks in public) could not have felt more despondent regarding his limited opportunities for space travel due to the skyrocketing costs.

He was tired of moonlighting at the pet shop which he thought was really for the birds.

He really hoped his space travel career would take off again soon. He thought it was such a blast and really felt like he didn't have the energy to launch a new one.

Due to the unorthodox nature of Hogswart, Harry Potter was never taught to spell correctly. His grammar is extremely poor. As a result, he has a lot of catching up to do and it will be quite a lengthy process. It isn't like anyone can just wave a magic wand in front of him for him to be able to get a firm grasp of it. Apparently this requirement will not be wa(i)ved.

Stephen's parents wished for him to use his Easter break to find opportunities that would help him explore potential careers.

He did not follow this advice and instead of taking advantage of such springboards, spent his spring bored.

Positively charged with the excitement of potentially electrifying earnings and the thrill of great risk, Johnny was very much looking forward to jump staring a new career hot-wiring cars.

I am currently seeking other alcohol enthusiasts to have regular meet-ups for ongoing spirited discussions.

My wife cannot get me to go to the dentist. It's like pulling teeth. If she can get me to go it will be one of her crowning achievements. I guess we'll cross that bridge when we get to it, but I wouldn't brace myself if I were you.

The former inmates were pleasantly surprised at the turn out for the state prison reunion.

Bob A. Richman, made sure to get everyone's contact information and having done well for himself, decided to make use of his unusually spacious home to throw a real(ly) killer party.

Everyone agreed in retrospect that although it was a great party, the traffic had truly been murder.

There was a brief moment when one of the guests slugged down a Coors Silver Bullet and shot off his mouth, but everyone was relieved to realize that it really wasn't a crime to state one's opinion with such long held serious convictions.

During the course of the evening, as conversation continued in Bob's courtyard, everyone ended up clicking so well just like in the old days and before too long, with so many exchanges, they even started finishing each other's sentences.

Weary of the political campaign, Cheryl stopped in at a karaoke joint for a drink and became enamored with a handsome talented singer named Ray.

She was so glad that he turned out to be single and they enjoyed many drinks together and seemed to share a real connection.

Cheryl really needed a night like this as she was so stressed out about the speech that, despite her objections, her campaign manager insisted she give next month.

In fact she was so stressed out that she made an appointment with a counselor.

As the counselor asked questions and took notes she paused for concern with the many references to Cheryl's Ray sing thoughts and pressured speech.

Until she understood more, she thought that she might need to be evaluated for bipolar disorder and be in the beginning stages of a manic episode.

Like many other Enterprising young men, just beginning to experience the joys of increasing profits, David decided to take an extended break from the paperwork, get up from his table at the Star Trek convention, put on his favorite music and do a bun dance.

Having often felt alienated and different from others, Joey's interest in space exploration hinged upon the potential discovery of other intelligent life on far away planets.

He thought he could fit in better with some other race and even be famous one day for being the first to make contact with the potential previously referenced Alien Nation.

Being outgoing and having access to lots of music are important assets to my music instruction business.

When customers feel like they want to connect with a friendly owner and their child is interested in a particular piece of music, but an arrangement suitable to their current skill level, a little extra version never hurt...

After many unusually bright summer days, our housekeeper decided to go to the half-off sunglasses sale that she saw advertised on television on her day off.

She thought she would have many fine and stylish choices, but instead found out that she had misunderstood what they had meant by half off.

She decided she didn't want to waste the trip and she purchased one that covered her right eye, which she felt was the one most sensitive to sunlight.

When it came to this new fashion trend, despite her meager salary, she really had it – maid / made in a shade.

The whole intent of the movie being produced was to share a sunny perspective on life with viewers. It centered on the simple life offered in a small mining town, now lost to so many in the fast-paced get ahead lifestyle of modern times.

However, there was a big problem that needed to be solved that threatened to undermine the successful production of this heart-warming film.

The casting director, Seymour Chances Castaway, had trouble turning down anyone who took the time to audition for a role, and as a result, the production was overcast for days on end.

Not liking to contemplate her own mortality, it was time to face facts. No more. Tisha (who was drop-dead gorgeous) stopped putting off pre-planning for her own inevitable demise.

It was a big step to finally be meeting with a pre-planning consultant at the urging of her family and the one with whom she was meeting had a great reputation. She had really earned / urned it.

Although the sales agent used no high pressure tactics, Tisha just felt put off and got up to leave saying "No thanks. Not right now. I'll pass."

Crystal Hill really loved to ski, but felt that too many of the employees at the resort were just too flaky.

Once she checked into the lodge where she was currently staying she had now been to all of them that she had planned on ever using.

She felt that in general, ski lodges' standards had really gone adrift and she tended to, when it came to recreational activities involving snow, bank on excellent customer service.

Crystal found the customer service she experienced during her first few days there to be atrocious.

She stormed to the front desk and with a frosty attitude, shouted at the manager, describing how she thought things should be when she came there to ski, lodging a series of complaints.

Later, in deep contemplation while staring up at the icy hills in the bright sunshine through the window in her room, upon reflection, she really took a good look at herself, and began to regret that she had to "go there" as a last resort.

Ann Teak was a young spry and attractive lady. Despite her modern taste in home décor, she went into the antique store and furnished the sexually deprived young man on the sales floor an opportunity to show Ann teak wood.

He thought there might be more in store, but he wasn't sure if that was the case though.

Maybe she wasn't buying it. Would see or wooden she?

There really seemed to be a certain mystery surrounding this Miss Teak.

Our friend Stacey took up with a new boyfriend, Adam. So as it turned out, we didn't know Stacey from Adam so to speak, but having known her longer and better, we ironically, knew Adam from Stacey.

After watching a special documentary on anorexia, the anxiety prone mother of a teenage girl had to be reassured that the chances of Twiggy developing the disorder were razor thin.

I refuse to raise 'er thin, she thought to herself, grateful that she had gotten the skinny on all of that, dipping into the support of a pool of experts on the subject.

She couldn't bear the thought of her daughter suffering so, especially in light of her recently obtained nautical instructor position and how swimmingly things seem to be going for her...

"I wouldn't sweat it too much", I said reassuringly to my dear friend during our regular afternoon walk one particularly warm summer's day.

When it came to the possibility of a promotion, I truly believed he was most certainly in the running.

I never let on that I had contacted his employer in hopes of helping him out by jogging his memory about my friend's great dedication to the company and the many significant contributions he had so selflessly made over the years.

Newspaper subscriptions are at an all-time low. These days, most professionals who work downtown are simply going to the internet on their lunch breaks in their modern, technologically cutting-edge, electronically rotating high rise office buildings to find out how many stories are unfolding.

Many parents, with the rapid rise in the use of electronic gadgets and smart phones, fear that without adequate supervision and guidance, they will end up leaving their children to their own devices.

"How are things going?" I asked my friend, Hunter Stool, who runs a successful plumbing business with his wife. "Different shit, different day" he concluded. "Still, I can't complain" he added. "The pipelines are filled to overflowing with many, many leads to the point that I'm always flush." "That's great!" I said. "How many kinds of leads are there?" I asked, concerned about the health of myself and others...

Upon further discussion, I was led to believe that there really was no cause for concern, and many others, having read the story were concerned for a short and similar, if not same, type of spell.

Truth be told, I'm a little envious of him and his rather tubby wife, Rose E. Stool. Unlike me, neither of them ever suffers from diarrhea, and as close and as organized as they both are with sinking / synching their schedules, they have their shit together nearly every morning. Sometimes, however, they lose it by the middle of the afternoon if the day proves draining enough.

In a freak accident, I lost a hand while playing cards. Having an extra ordinary mind I have two thoughts on the subject.

First of all, having learned my lesson, I should no longer be driven to the clubs, but then again, on the other hand it may be a matter of safety that I am.

When I was in high school, I felt really bad for one of my dear friends, whose mother, Patience Lack-King, constantly berated him, making him feel like he could never get an A rating in her overbearing and critical eyes.

When interviewing candidates for my music teaching positions, I usually feel more secure about hiring those who give very measured responses to my questions.

One of the employees at the bumper replacement shop, Chrome-O-Zone is missing. He is described as a quirky fellow with a lot of unusual tics.

I grabbed my cellphone and quickly pressed "0", hoping it could work some kind of magic, but nothing happened.

Having often shed light upon the downside of his furniture building business, I was not really that floored when Maxx told me that he was looking for a career change.

He had couched it many different ways recently, but then preferred to table the discussion.

His main concern was finding a sufficient enough alternate source of income to help him shape his future and cushion the blow so that the change will not end up pulling the rug out from under him.

Proud that his YouTube video had gone viral, the boy shared the news with his pediatrician who then warned him to make sure it didn't become bacterial.

When it came to his strange obsession with exacerbating his flatulent tendencies, there really was no telling just how far Ted would go...

He couldn't understand why dairy products never had typical effects on him, so he went to Google and found some interesting related information about what made some foods very iron"y" and it was thus that he was able to supplement his understanding as well as his efforts.

There is no denying that men who suffer from premature ejaculation experience a number of similar shortcomings in their intimate relationships.

There was just no telling what would be going on with his girlfriend.

Sometimes she just got into such an unpleasant and perplexing moo(e)d in which she always seemed to be having a cow.

The very talented magician ran such a fast paced and engaging show for the first half hour that when he amazed the audience with his levitation illusion, they were confused when the pace suddenly slowed as he remained on this part of the act seemingly forever.

As time began to creep along he really left them up in the air in a state of total suspense.

I know a woman, Miss Paran Partigan, who was such a yenta that she not only gets involved in the kind of match-making that could set the world on fire, but she also tends to give advice when she thinks it might be time for couples to break up and move on.

Such was the case with the particular woman with whom she was speaking with now. "You know what I think, honey?" she asked. "OK" replied the despondent woman. "I'm going to give you my two scents."

She handed the lady two small bottles and she, understandably, asked "What are these for?" Smiling, the yenta said "You told me you just wish he would go away. That it's just getting too painful for you. These are repellents", she explained. "Problem solved." She said gleefully.

If you've ever seen a square dance, it seems ironic just how many hip movements occur above the waist for such an otherwise dull affair.

Do you gather as much? And if so for what kinds of events?

Did you happen to catch the talented vocal performance of Miss Singh at the Veteran Affairs' P.O.W. – M.I.A. benefit? Boy, I'm tell ya' you should have seen Miss Singh in action!

As the newest member of this terrific book club, I am very interested in starting a new chapter, and wanted to find a partner who is on the same page as me regarding this to help me to head it up. It could be a great partnership. Just mark my words.

The first book which I just recently completed that I'd like to recommend for discussions is a real page turner entitled

"All of My Love." It's about the secret, never before publicized brief romance between Jimmy Page and Tina Turner.

Never having taken Tina for a pot smoker, I was a bit surprised when there was a reference to them taking a boat river cruise together and smoking a joint out on the deck, saying they had decided to roll it on a river.

Unbeknownst to many, cowboy Bob was a talented mathematician and sometimes served as a substitute teacher, when he wasn't busy attending rodeos.

As he turned the page in the textbook to lead the class, he was pleasantly surprised to see that the lesson at hand where the regular teacher had last left off was all about how to round up.

William was always an ambitious child and also was the sort to always try to do the right thing. When he grew up, it was no surprise to anyone when he began his own enterprise: a large department store he named Bill of Goods.

After many years of success, William wished to sell the store and retire. It was not long before he met with a well-capitalized investor who was interested in making the purchase.

Seeing what a good and honest man William was, his trust was soon earned by the potential investor. By the time he left the meeting, the possible buyer had nearly made a decision and was sure he could get a fair deal when William sold him his Bill of Goods.

A single friend of mine had been flirting with an attractive bank teller and former crossing guard for a number of weeks who seemed to give him mixed signals. Finally he asked her if she would consider going out with him. She answered "I'm off on Friday." "So you can go out with me to lunch on Friday then?" he asked. "I told you I'm not telling" she answered.

Refusing to simply cooperate and blend in at the coffee shop, my Aunt Tenna really stands out.

Due to the governor's suspected misappropriation of funds, many county residents are deeply concerned about how the next several days will go without enough money for the usual response to moderate snow storms, let alone the blizzard that is being predicted. No one seems amused about the real snow job that is expected to be uncovered as the evidence keeps piling up.

Despite how tiring the process is bound to be, many, as this apparently growing, unusual political snow storm hits, championed by Ms. Deeds, are calling for his personal removal as punishment for his otherwise, entirely much too inconsequential misdeeds.

Many of my friends are well aware of my penchant for chiming in, as appropriate, on my mini harmonica during our mutually enjoyed karaoke nights out.

What I am not sure that I told everyone is that a couple I have been friends with for many years gave it to me for Christmas and had found it at a shop one day while riding their rented mini-bike on a much enjoyed Minnie vacation in Disney World.

Every once in a while, some kind of abrasive character will show up uninvited to an otherwise pleasant musical jam gathering.

I tend not to let such things bother me, and in fact, one such character recently showed up.

In hopes of keeping the peace and harmony, I grabbed my xylophone stick and, against his large metal collar for some, as of yet undisclosed medical condition, decided to ever so gently (w)ring his neck.

In light of some scary economic indicators, an emergency political meeting was held in Washington D.C.

The general public is not exactly sure what to think, but given the rumors of a second meeting there really may be a re-session at hand...

It is my understanding that operating a restaurant can be challenging, especially in terms of staffing. Due to the rotation of menus, the return of out of state college students to school in the fall and complaints of bland food in a somewhat desperate move, a local restaurant owner, Constance D. Change, placed an ad for a seasoned, seasonal seasoner.

Personally, I think it could be a recipe for disaster. Not knowing much about operating a restaurant, I could be wrong.

The thought of it leaves a bad taste in my mouth.

Excited and somewhat nervous about her plans, a decidedly very funny seamstress, Cher A. Curtain, closed her fabric store to pursue a new career in stand-up comedy.

With the air of confidence indicative of successful entrepreneurs, she staged herself for success, certain that she had enough material.

Seems stress did not get the better of her and in fact, years later, I have heard reports that she's laughing all the way to the bank.

Trixie had been an assistant to magician Happy Carver for many, many years, and was worried that they seemed to be drawing smaller crowds, despite the great artistry of their shows. In fact, though Happy had never discussed shortening her hours - she feared this would soon be the case.

These fears grew even further when she happened to see him out in public last time she was shopping and he never returned her smile and wave from a distance. In reality, he did not see her, but she was afraid he was pretending.

Due to his preoccupation with the decline in business, this same scenario occurred several times over the following months, although about half the time, he did spot her and waved back.

Finally she just couldn't take it anymore and in the middle of the show as he was getting ready to do the saw the lady in half trick she became very emotional and accused him, in front of the audience of attempting to reduce the number of times her saw her in half.

While at the bar, the single long time astronomer was absolutely certain that he could tell a scope from a merely cursory glance better than those of other professions.

Although it was located in a quaint little rural town, the management of the mill had gradually shifted to a much more educated crowd of sophisticated elites who felt strongly that the local riff-raff, whom they considered run of the mill should never run the mill.

Penny Pincher had been a medical practitioner for many years and had a notorious reputation for having all kinds of additional and obscure, inadequately explained charges itemized on her patients' bills.

Because of the low incidence of white collar crimes brought to trial, let alone, resulting in prosecution, many in the town felt vindicated when she was found guilty of financial malfeasance.

Even more surprisingly, the judge drew upon a newly passed law, astonishingly allowing for sentences as severe as capital punishment for white collar business crimes depending upon the severity and longevity of said wrongdoings.

Penny Pincher met these requirements. To the delight of many, new elements of the law came to light which allowed for a public execution and the judge, tired of white collar professionals' escape from justice, deemed such a venue.

The new law called for the punishment to meet, but not exceed the crime, and allowed for creative and unusual methods to be employed.

Because of this being the first implementation of this new law, all of her victims attended and her execution became a national multi-media event.

In reflection of and accounting for all of this change, the methods of execution were deemed to be in compliance with the law.

With the use of a completely filled dump truck, as the countdown continued and the suspense built Penny inevitably ended her 4th quarter, in a surprising final act of retribution that ended her life.

As the contents of the dump truck were strategically emptied upon her, Penny was literally nickeled and dimed to death, and to the shock of many when the story hit the papers, apparently in the presence of a direct descendant of the person who had originally coined the expression.

Sadly, Faith had fallen in love with a secretly sinister cardiologist who found the perfect way to melt her heart when she least expected it.

I watched another tear jerker yesterday with my wife. It was the sad story of two gay hairstylists Neil and Ben Dover who not only had style, but had really been through thick and thin together. It had everything in it from their adoption of a beautiful baby boy from Greece to a trying medical emergency when Neil's side burns and he has to be rushed to the hospital where he has a close shave with death.

After years, due to a lot of circumstantial stress, a break-up inevitably ensues when they decide to part ways permanently. Sadly they get overly snippy with one another and rather than getting to the root of their problems, end up splitting hairs over minor issues that could have easily been brushed aside.

The most heart-wrenching part is watching the custody battle over Harry. It's so impossible to pick sides and there's no way anyone with a heart watching this could say that they could not see how the situation really cut both ways as the judge begins combing through all of his notes to render a decision.

Although I'm not an overly religious man, the testimony is quite compelling and emotional when Neil, on bended knee pours his heart out and states how he should not fear, knowing that God has counted all of the hairs on our heads.

In the Bible it is said that God wanted to make more of himself in some way shape or form as he was feeling lonely.

With no one around yet to say anything like "way to go God" or "atta God, good job" he gave Himself an "atta me" and it was thus, in the spirit of his original idea that spirit took the form of flesh.

With little competition yet, He really left them in the dust, at least initially, but having been the first one on the block, and with a seemingly perpetual need for credit, everything always seemed to return to that.

At the sandwich shop, things were really running behind and an increasingly impatient customer eventually starting screaming at an employee "when can I get my sub, dude?" in a less than subdued manner.

Skye is one of the most grounded musicians I have ever met. She has a lot to keep organized about as a flight attendant with long hours who spends most of her days with her head up in the clouds.

Many hopeful candidates have applied for her position should it ever become vacant, but given her excellent attendance and performance, if they are relying strictly on this elusive opportunity, then they must be really flighty and are sure to find themselves strapped and waiting on the wings.

I took a picture of my wife in the kitchen doing ordinary household chores using a broom and decided to post it to Facebook. I knew it was unrealistic to expect all posts or picture shares to leave a broad-sweeping impression, I thought to myself. But this one though, I believed, despite how ordinary it was, would do just that.

The funeral for the victim of the politically controversial murder was just now taking place. Seemingly, every personality with their own political shows like Sean Hannity and Rachel Maddow had something to say.

How crazy the timing turned out to be at this sadly political media circus. Just as they lowered the casket and the mourners grabbed their small shovels they got the dirt on her, much to the delight or dismay of (depending on their political orientation) all those television news personalities who punned it.

An unexpected and very heated political debate that no one would have ever conceived of developed at the local Planned Parenthood.

The coordinators of the safe sex and birth control education committee were launching a new program called Condom Nation.

Many conservative Christians who were against premarital sex and birth control itself even between married couples, felt so strongly that they protested outside with signs that more than insinuated the role of Planned Parenthood in being accomplices in sending many people, in their condemnation, straight to hell.

The coordinators of the program stared out the window in disbelief from the part of the building specially designated for the distribution of condoms known as The Rubber Room.

The protest soon became violent and the police showed up and made several arrests.

During the hearings for these protesters, many were deemed to have mental health problems, and so as a direct result of their outrage about the program, wound up (they really were) in mental health facilities where they were, upon occasion, placed in their very own special rubber rooms.

Injuries at raves appear to once again be on the rise. Many of our youth, after such an experience, depending on the severity of their injury, feel very strongly about speaking out and seeking media attention.

One such victim was able to successfully have a segment aired on the nightly news. The reporter was briefed before the live segment was filmed about the young girl's shattered hip bone and all of the medical complications that arose as she limped towards recovery.

The reporter, sympathetically pointed towards the reformed rave enthusiast's injured side to get the conversation started.

"It's that hip, right?" asked the reporter. The young lady said "no, it's not that hip at all and that's what I'm here to tell all of the young people whom I hope to convince to never get involved in this pathetic scene I once thought was so cool."

The woman made a reference to having been to a Beatles concert and then said "Boy I really date myself." "How's that going?" I asked.

The police were contacted about a report of flying saucers. "That's a matter for the local media" said Sgt. Pepper. He took a few notes and called the local media with the information. When they arrived, the media personnel were bewildered and confused as they stood at the tragic scene of a woman who, at the end of her rope, had hung herself after so many years of domestic abuse.

As a result, a media story was put together to raise public awareness of programs for victims of domestic abuse, designed to intervene before such desperate ends are reached. The story really questioned whether police training programs needed to be more comprehensive given that the nature of the call that the police department had first received should not have been treated as such an alien concept.

In order to promote greater productivity, the construction company is holding an official sta(i)ring contest.

So far it's going reasonably OK, at least for those who stare well, but a few mentally unstable employees, who put themselves under much self-imposed pressure, went off the rails and wound up landing in a local mental hospital.

Apparently, the rate of stare cases is climbing.

Being new to foot fetishes, and unbeknownst to either of them, the woman's clumsy new young lover, Lefty Wright-Foote in an overemotional reaction related to his growing split personality disorder, was totally beside himself when he realized that he had really gotten off on the wrong foot with her.

The charlatan psychic's patrons were often in a state of grief and did not give thought to things as obvious as a mirror when it came to wanting to believe in the paranormal.

Sadly her newest customer's husband had just passed away a few weeks ago. The bereaved woman sat facing the psychic holding her list of various facts that, if referenced, would convince her that the medium had true gifts.

She sat with her paper, written only on her own side, and waited patiently as the medium made (eye) contact with The Other Side, astounded at her accuracy.

It really was amazing she thought, as she reflected on what a great image the medium was making for herself, and glad she had resorted to such a strategic location.

Fred Flintstone really needed some brake work done, but word on the street was he had really been dragging his feet on it.

Hopefully he will take care of this soon so as to avoid any accidents that could leave him in the Rubble.

My wife said I spoke too much so she bought me a unicycle, thereby back pedaling on her previous promise to purchase a bike for me. Due to inflation, it cost way more than she expected, leaving my balance in jeopardy, and I fear possibly seeing bloody red with only the slightest miscalculation, but now rim jobs are no longer out of the question. No pressure.

Life expectancy is shorter in Cuban years. So people's ages are raised to the 3rd power.

This reminds me of a sad story where a 3 year old toddler, who already showed serious signs of musical genius unexpectedly joined the Forever 27 Club. As a result, he never got to finish preparing his rendition, being as precocious as he was, of "When I'm Sixty Four" by The

Beatles which he had planned to sing and play for his mother on his 4th birthday.

Feeling neglected by her husband whose orchestra she had played in for years, she sat sadly playing her violin during the performance.

As she sat, ironically she thought to herself, playing first fiddle, she entertained fears that he was secretly fiddling around with the second violinist whom she sat next to....

A medical documentary was being filmed in real time and at the moment was focusing on a critical surgery.

As one of the intern assistants was holding a surgical knife and awaiting the head surgeon's further instructions, the director was heard to say "cut right there."

The assistant thought he had heard the head surgeon's voice. This Englishman's bloody mistake proved tragic, and unfortunately a terrible and otherwise avoidable loss has occurred.

General Specific was notorious for giving contradictory orders, and in so doing, ended up leading his troops into yet another civil war.

Even though business has been picking up significantly, I have needed to tighten my belt lately due to my progress with my diet and exercise program.

Just like my belt and the soon to be hung criminal with a freakishly tiny penis awaiting the floor to drop with the noose around his neck, (he was left hanging for quite some time due to some technical difficulties in executing his execution), I just wanted to keep you in the loop.

Dr. Cummings had been a birth control educator for many years, but he finally decided it was time to pull out and start a different career.

I know a politician, Lucky Farmer who, ironically, went against the grain whenever he voted in favor of pro-agribusiness legislation.

A man, who remained anonymous for a long time, (Justin D. Law) kept calling my business office to complain every time a round of 100 signs went out to promote our in-home piano, guitar and voice lessons.

He really harped on us for using this method of drumming up interest in our services and really wanted to teach us a lesson.

People who cannot pun well really need help. Their words plays are so terrible that I don't even know what their pun"ish" meant / should be.

EVEN MORE UNEXPECTED MUSINGS COME

FO(U)RTH:

AN EXPLORATION OF EVEN MORE COLORFUL REFLECTIONS WITHIN MY GRAY MATTER

(Trust me – they really do....)

After Section 3, you would have thought I had gotten it all out of my system, but apparently there was even more that I had entered into my database...

As the title says, even more came fo(u)rth and thus I felt it my duty to share additional musings that I hope will be enriching for everyone...especially me.

It seems to never take me very long to be able to recharge enough for new material. With today's technology, it's often instantaneous and at what I believe, a fair price for admission to the carnival that is my mind.

The ole' factory continues to produce more food for thought yielding even more dollars and scents typical of the smell of sweet success.

I truly hope that you will enjoy my mind's somewhat convoluted contents to your heart's content...

SECTION 4

I had a table at a flea market and was hoping to make some money that day. A very curious lesbian woman came by to look at my junk, but quickly left saying she wasn't buying. About 20 minutes later she returned and I told her, "It might not be so appealing right now, but don't worry....it'll grow on ya!"

Lacking in both libido and humor as well as corporate values, I drifted off to sleep. I slept funny, but woke up as stiff as a Board (of Directors).

I WROTE THIS ONE ON THE FLY

A little baby fly, hungry for his parents' approval continued to practice his skills, in hopes of gaining their accolades. Much to the dismay of one of the homeowners, So King, the baby fly was using a door handle on the inside of the bathroom as his take off point.

On the farthest side from this take off point lay the freshly drawn bath that So was planning on enjoying shortly after finishing up an unexpected phone call...

With great exuberance, the baby fly suddenly flew off the handle, and with sufficient effort, got past his previous sticking point, fervently landing himself in a lot of hot water and thus gaining the praise of his parents he had so longed for...but in the process, getting So King slightly wet.

At least this is what her husband, Joe King told me and, as an accountant with a professional attachment to helping everyone maintain their balance correctly, he is not one to try to make a splash with humorous hyperbole or pull anyone's leg.

As I continue to enjoy pouring out all of my writing and ideas into this book, I find myself longing for some comradery with other authors.

I think it would be great if we could form some kind of community. At least for those of us who could afford a second home or be flexible enough to move...

It would be a great change of scene for us creative and more prolific types to be of support to each other as we continue to author and publish more and more original and creative material under the auspices of our own special writer's block.

Studies have proven that children with watches wind up happier. Bravo!

Let's give them a second hand!!!

I was so flattered when a very famous and well accomplished word smith looked at some of my work and the old pro found much of it quite meaningful.

The sign-language impaired participants in the Silent Auction felt a sense of gratitude when I showed up in my unusually loud shirt and was able to assist with some of my knowledge. It really came in handy. You would think such an event would be boring, (supposedly no holes in that argument), but truth be told it was a total scream.

I suggested to management that in the future, they offer courses proactively to expected participants, but they rejected my motion(s) and it only fell upon deaf ears...

Sitting along the wall of the fountain in the center of the mall I said to my friend resignedly, "Oh well, what are you going to do?" "I don't know, what do you think?" suddenly boomed a sardonic voice that welled-up within the fountain, much to our surprise "Probably just stay stuck here accepting random pennies from well-wishers."

It was apparent that the restaurant owner, Larry was really getting fed up with his manager. He was so terrible about being proactive with keeping things ordered. As essential items continued to run in short supply, despite his numerous talks with him, so did his patience.

From the look on Larry's face, I knew without a doubt that as he poured himself a soda and added ice, that as he reached for his sipping aid that it really was the last straw.

Suddenly, in the middle of such discursive thoughts, the bachelorette on the beach suddenly spotted a tan gent.

When he returned her glance, she felt it a sure sign that she should introduce herself. They met and developed a flip-flop relationship. Before they knew it, they were married and had cosigned on a mortgage, leading to massive confusion amongst the divorce lawyers as they divorced and remarried each other three times so far to date.

A young local gastroenterologist, Dr. Perry Stals is working on a universal remedy for constipation. In gratitude for his uncle Ob, who had paid his medical school tuition in full, Dr. Perry plans to call the remedy, once complete, Ob's Cure and hopes that it will ultimately become a household name.

It appears that adult ADHD is becoming an epidemic with public health and safety implications. Just last week there were 3 more cases of derailed trains from engineers each of whom admitted they (were) dis-tracked it.

Without some serious intervention, this whole sector of the public transportation industry could become a total(led) train wreck. Parenthetically, I believe someone should make sure their lights are on. Perhaps, we should even capitalize on this idea as we reach this important crossroads, as I truly believe it, at the very least ties loosely into the problem.

In fact, we are seeing a real ripple effect of untreated ADHD children growing up and putting others at risk as well.

Another recent headline describes how a distracted cruise ship captain, having gone completely overboard in regards to the neglect of his responsibilities, was having his cap sized at an extremely crucial moment, resulting in a catastrophic ship wreck. Survivors are still picking up the pieces.

On the verge of filing for divorce, Mike was so fed up with his wife's failure to perform domestic duties. "The witch" he thought. Next time the kitchen floor needs sweeping, I'm going to take the broom, stick it up her ass and then call my lawyer.

When all was said and done, in the end, despite her lack of domestic skills, she wound up being one of the best housekeepers ever. She made a totally clean break, largely because of her spotless record with the authorities, which really left him in the dust... helping her to clean up well while he stood there at the hearing in clean and neatly pressed appropriate clothing, but a very spotty criminal record.

The newlywed couple, excited about their home decor upgrades, could not wait to share a picture of their new lighting fixture on Facebook. A completely innocent, yet rather shady lamp post. It's really strange when you think about it that such a mundane share could actually really brighten up someone's day.

It is inherently difficult for most of us to comprehend the reality of the Holocaust. We simply cannot comprehend how the typical Nazi could not see the inhumanity of his actions.

The human limb removal specialist went on and on about how, during his long procedures, he timed his ingestion of food to maintain his focus and stamina during these difficult and very time-consuming procedures. He came up with a formula and for every so many per sever, ate a specified amount of protein rich food.

A woman once told me that she met a physician who seemed to have some kind of other worldly spiritual healing powers.

My wife and I considered doing a 69, but then we realized we would probably end up with opposing points of view.

The unsophisticated salon worked entertained the most mundane of thoughts as she waxed Phil O. Sophical.

I grew increasingly weary of this seemingly fruitless mission which, in waters more suitable for white water rafting, was rapidly getting old.

As I continued searching for the allegedly mythical landmArk by boat, my zest for life faced a semantically framed internal struggle when I unexpectedly reached the Fountain of youth in Asia.

I want to avoid concentration camp this summer. That would really kill me.

However, my tutor Patty really has some nice buns and I really need a break, as I'm feeling a bit toasted at the moment.

I'm really hungry with the full knowledge that I must buckle down soon and thought that these tutoring sessions would really help me get myself in gear and would prove to be the perfect vehicle for my academic improvement.

In the meantime, I need some rest and would also like to order a double bacon cheeseburger.

I need help with this main course and I feel like, otherwise, it's going to give me a heart attack.

I've got a lot on my plate. Perhaps I've even already bitten off more than I can chew.

This could be a serious matter, so I'm not just saying things or asking for a full-throated endorsement in jest.

I could really use some encouragement as I am starting to think about just sticking a fork in it.

A(_)side from all of that, to be completely honest, studying French fries my brain.

A terrible tragedy was recently spotlighted at the Ringling Brother's Barnum and Bailey show, when the lion suddenly escaped from his cage and went right for the juggler.

It was quite a horrific spectacle for those who witnessed how the outfit's original vision had been seriously trampled upon and sadly became the white elephant in the room.

Beforehand the entire cast of characters had felt that they had everything sewn up tight, roped into thinking all would be pulled off quite well - including the clothing of the nudist trapeze artist.

Instead, the tragedy has become the focus of a media circus.

Simply amazing what a feat it is and how many hoops you have to jump through before a reporter will really listen to you and give you audience.

Even, the stunt man who had been scheduled next to escape handcuffed from a locked water tank had the sinking feeling that it would be a long while before things would go swimmingly for the company again, as they had for many, many years.

Time and traditional newspapers will show how this story unfolds. Can you see the big picture?

Please pardon my extensive play on words. I think it's just in my blood.

I really have to let it all out. Even if it becomes the death of me.

They've just built a new cruise ship specifically custom tailored to accommodate passengers with phobias related to sailing aptly named Chicken of the Sea.

Hopefully this will work out better than the Good Ship Lollipop that was built with the very same concept, but didn't turn out to be a lifesaver or make the kind of splash that it was supposed to due to the poor training of the staff in dealing with the passenger's known anxieties.

Sadly, it turned out that the panic stricken passengers felt like total suckers and my heart just sank when I first learned how the employees of the cruise ship really did not have the skills to help better anchor those suffering from panic attacks with a greater sense of calm or make them feel like they could slide into a safe space...

Even worse, with their employee's high call out rate for such specialized cruises relying heavily on good staffing: no shows.

Feeling mad horny (though both were in terrific spirits) and needing a break from the never ending circus at home with the kids, the couple hired a baby sitter and hoped for an impromptu overnight hotel stay to get away from it all.

Carefully balancing himself on his unicycle, his wife got up on his shoulders to allow him to transport them for the first leg of the trip.

He was so happy she had agreed to switch places for the second half of the trip.

It was always so much more fun when they each got to take turns going to town on each other.

When they got there, unfortunately no rooms were available. Despite the seeming futility of the exercise, the couple, in retrospect, somehow found the journey oddly satisfying.

IT MAY COME AS A SURPRISE GIVEN MY VERBOSITY, AVERAGE PHYSICAL STATURE AND GENERAL DISPOSITION BUT I AM GOING TO BE SHORT WITH MY READERS ONCE AGAIN

Now that I have worn all of my hats out, when it comes to all of these random, creative musings in my head, with the holidays just around the corner it's really getting to be old hat(s).

As a white collar professional who tends to dress casually, as hard as it was to picture, I was pleased to develop, with little to no film on (I was freshly showered at the time), a rather amazing ability to look quite blue collar, despite wearing such drab colors and a brownish-gray shirt.

Hopefully, at this point in time, with no musical facility whatsoever, I should be completely booked in every way possible and should really be cleaning up.

In fact, I once again visited the controversial psychic that has been referred to in this book and she said that once she had a clear reading, she believed that by Jan. I to(u)r.

I entertained yet a 3rd business idea, but it is now patently being kept under lock and key. Among other things, it would help some professional car salesmen keep their trade marked with significant and helpful changes.

It is an app that would track their leads and sales, but with more detailed analysis and specialized charts / graphs than usual to increase sales, retention, repeat business and lead flow.

I was thinking of scrapping the whole idea, but when I go on my book tour, if the psychic's predictions are correct, I can perhaps sell you the writes (rights) (to) (of) my auto graph.

Rick O'Shea felt truly blessed that he had managed to escape the ravages of war and arrived home safely after years of battle, seemingly somehow, completely impervious to bullet wounds of any kind.

The Lorax, tiring of his whole rant against the anti-environmentalist businessman (Chip D. Woods) for one of the first times in his life, found himself completely stumped.

Miss Fickle felt like it was going to be a real game changer when she met Mr. Wright. After all, they had put all of their cards on the table and he seemed to be (unlike some of her previous boyfriends) playing with a full deck.

As a world renown chess champion he was certainly flush and loving kids as much as she did, she really didn't mind at all that he had a full house of children from his previous marriage, all of whom were characters in their own right.

They enjoyed going to the same clubs, the dogs had been spayed, he had a heart of gold and she certainly couldn't complain about the diamond engagement ring.

She knew it was a numbers game and felt strongly that if she played her cards right she could easily overlook the fact that he was slight of hand, even though she knew it sometimes made it challenging at times for him to really get a grip on himself.

She only had one thing left to do, and a voice inside her head kept nagging "check mate before you wind up with a house of cards." She finally followed her gut feeling, and confirmed her deepest fears and broke-up with him when she found out that her now once-beloved chess champion had a checkered past. A few weeks later he died, apparently of a broken heart, having simply been unable to pick up the pieces and fearing that when it came to any possible future romances, the cards were simply stacked against him and it would really be of no use to try and roll the dice again.

Some weeks later Miss Fickle received the news from a mutual friend and was incredibly despondent in hearing that he had cashed his chips in.

I still remember Sandy Crotches from the beach side commune who was trying to make waves in the food industry with an eye towards a growing need for more organic products.

This beatnik woman had a great recipe for a hip pie, but it was difficult to get many of her fellow residents in the commune, even after having put the exact right words together to eat it because it strangely made them feel, in their lack of comprehension, like cannibals that were eating their own kind.

With all of the telephone solicitations asking for donations for various worthy causes, it's enough to start to annoy even the most cheerful among us. After all, it was enough to leave Phil Anthro pissed.

Ann Ticipation was recently recognized as a Zen Master with an exceedingly unusually strong ability to stay mindful and fully in the present.

In hopes of attracting more customers, the bakery is thinking of employing a roll model.

As such a limited part-time job, the management, in an attempt to butter up potential candidates with a questionable past, will be completely unconcerned with anything in the new hire's personal life.

Beautiful women run in my family. Often at nearly 90 miles an hour after they spot me. If felt good to finally admit that. It's truly like a real weight off of my shoulders.

Thrifty environmentalists are always interested in saving a few bucks whenever possible.

POT LUCK SUGGESTIONS FOR THE PARTY AT OUR HOUSE –

MEMORIAL WEEKEND -2017

ANOTHER UPLIFTING PARTY IF WE GUEST CORRECTLY

We know that things always work out well with guests bringing something to share. So the following is to help give ideas to those of you who have not joined us before based on our previous gatherings:

Percussionists often bring the drumsticks. Our more pessimistic guests often bring sour grapes. Our most wanted guests (often unknowingly) bring chips on their shoulders, putting all of us at risk for the police showing up due to such tracking devices.

One lady brought a really shitty meal, but she meant well. What were we to do? Sue 'er?

Another guest, born into wealth, but rather stingy, only brought a gray V for the alphabet soup, but finally loosened up during karaoke when he suddenly added the mashed potato to the mix...

Those who like to chide others and haven't for a while often bring a few spare ribs

Unlikely guests, the Spice Girls will bring condom mints (if they show)

Our Turkish friends will bring some turkey

The Swiss, cheese

A few are expected to fly in from Chile bringing some cold beverages

Our guitarists and singers always bring the jam

...Our most humorous guests will spike the punch, greatly contributing to nearly unending punch lines.

Mostly Neil Goldberg, Phil Woolfson, Mark J. Gross and I, as usual, will provide some very uncanny & saucy tastes to the mix....and lastly, we can always count on some unlikely guest with great care and pride to bring some obscure and exotic dish. Last year, for instance, someone gave a rat's ass.

Stan Ding was passionate about so many political causes, but opted out of the sit-in.

A woman went to see a therapist, feeling like her intimate relationships always failed in the long run. She laid down, not sure exactly how to couch her perception of the reasons for her despondency.

She then began to describe her current relationship with a carpenter whom she loved dearly, but felt, just like her previous boyfriends, just got hammered too often, stopped screwing her, and she feared in conjunction with a gut-wrenching feeling, that he wasn't really being on the level with her and that it was reaching a point that things would never get patched-up again.

In the future she plans to be much more cautious about carefully laying a solid foundation to help better cement her future relationships.

From geographically remote areas, a scientist and a fisherman both simultaneously exclaimed "Fishin' accomplished!"

As happy as they both were, they each retained that glowing feeling for quite some time...

Feeling lately like my connection to others has been hanging by a thread due to distracting ambitions I have decided to start a whole new chapter in my life.

I am now seeking social climbers who would be interested in hanging out and excitedly taking stock of and exchanging fishy stories with a number of cliffhangers of ever-increasing scale.

In hopes of salvaging Trump's presidency, a few members of his base decided to create a Go Fund Me Page. I suggested they entitle the page: "Fund A Mentally Challenged POTUS!"

Tony Orlando and Dawn are seeing a resurgence in vintage record sales of their 45 hit "Knock Three Times".

Many attribute this trend to a connection with the Sheldon Cooper character of the Big Bang Theory, who, in his quirky austerity, knocked knock-knock jokes, and in symbolic protest adopted his signature door rap.

I apologize that I had forgotten to mention that my old friend, and fellow punster, Irie Pete from Jamaica and I are planning a trip to Ireland.

Although he prefers reggae music, he is open to other forms of music as well.

We plan on hitting a few pubs, and he, being single hopes to get jiggy with some Gaelic music, hopefully in effort to connect with any attractive single young women who might be interested in some straight licks from a lead guitarist who is rumored to be an oral expert.

He is quite a cunning linguist and given that English is not his native language, you could say he is really adept with a foreign (far in) tongue.

UNSURE IF THERE IS CAUSE TO FRET OR NOT

As an essential part of their rehabilitation, the mental hospital provided music therapy for their patients.

Being quite adamant about ensuring that the patients received the full benefit, one particularly popular music therapist was questionably let go for making sure he persisted in his efforts until each patient finally snapped.

Although the musician in question always dressed casually, there are rumors of a suit, centering around the possibility of him having previously undiscovered sadistic tendencies.

Many are beginning to point their fingers and explain why of all people, they were picking on the guitarist.

Ultimately, time will tell just how confining his efforts may really turn out to be.

As is often the case, many have different opinions regarding whether he should ultimately be barred or rewarded with a standing Ovation.

Personally, I think he has been amazingly and efficiently effective, often fostering great therapeutic value for many patients in nearly no time flat.

Why don't they just clock him?

After a super long debate that ran through the night, those who did and did not believe in the resurrection of Jesus Christ stopped feeling so cross with one another and finally agreed that there was an ultimate point in time in which there was quite a stretch (but according to one side it was followed by a yawn and an exit of the tomb).

When I first heard (about how) Wendy's Baconator (was being promoted on a television advertisement), I was half asleep and thought it was a public service announcement referring to some scary and unexplainably bizarre new crime wave sandwiched between more typical commercials.

A rather self-important physicist claimed that he was able to defy the laws of physics by having a pillow that had both sides down.

It was really a crime the way he was so self-absorbed and continuously attempting to self-aggrandize himself.

This may have just been some sort of half-hearted attempt at pillow talk, meant to impress his fiance who was studying to become a cardiologist, but the recently hired largely sexually repressed female Muslim authorities, many of whom were former shepherds, having caught wind of this claim from an established meteorologist fleeced him, but despite their thinly veiled attempts to cross the line with their methods, simply could not get a rise out of him.

I once met a red-headed phrenologist who, in her youth, was very Type A about her school work and always followed the summer reading recommendations.

In essence, she was a red-head who read ahead and read heads.

The athlete more or less operated as an independent contractor, and as such, was entitled to a fair amount of income tax shelters.

He felt like his new accountant was a team player and was so impressed with his run down of all of the uniform codes that he felt comfortable with all of his recommendations, even beginning with his first piece of advice (:) right off / write off the bat.

His trust had been won and the athlete couldn't have been more comfortable having scored such an impressive professional to tackle the job for him.

The possibility of a potentially horrific crisis suddenly crossed my mind, when, in reflecting on how much as of late, the world seems to be my oyster, I suddenly remembered my fatal allergy to shell fish, and completely panicked at the thought of becoming, just like the late Shelly Fisher, merely a shell of my former self.

Being in the music instruction business, I suddenly felt like a hypocrite when I found myself irritated that my printer had just started jamming.

MY DEAR SON, STEPHEN JUST DAYS BEFORE GRADUATING FROM NEWTOWN HIGH SCHOOL IN JUNE 2017.

STEPHEN WAS AWARDED 26 COLLEGE CREDITS FOR BEING THE VERY FIRST & ONLY STUDENT IN HIS SCHOOL TO PASS

THE CompTIA A+ CERTIFICATION EXAM

Mark J Gross Photography 2017

I would really like to introduce you here to my invisible dog, Reality.

Please be careful if you ever have the chance to meet him in person.

REALITY BITES!

GETTING READY TO WALK THE DOG IN PUBLIC

CERTAIN THAT NO ONE WILL EVER SEE IT

I'VE BEEN AROUND THE BLOCK A FEW TIMES ALREADY

He is a powerful dog, and for the most part I let him do as he pleases, but being unable to see him, I must keep him on a very tight leash. If he ever managed to unleash himself, it would, in my point of view, almost be as if Reality had somehow disappeared into dog-gone thin air.

At that point, reconnecting me with Reality could require extreme measures and prove challenging until I finally fully grasp all of Reality's hidden dimensions. After such a scare, with him having been exposed to the potential perils of this dog eat dog world, surely I'd put him in the dog house and seriously contemplate new ways of helping to ensure that Reality remain completely under my command.

My very first introduction to Reality occurred rather late in life at a flea market last year and I must say, the owner, who was putting on quite a dog and pony show at his booth fetched a pretty penny for him. At first he was a bit cagey about discussing the cost, but then he really wouldn't let me haggle with him at all, so when it came to getting top dollar he was just like a dog with a bone.

Sadly, there is no logical way to tag Reality on Facebook for any future identification purposes. Before thinking that through, I had considered sharing a post, but was really on the fence about it. I must find a way to ensure that Reality is here to stay. I love my dog so much and would be completely devastated if I permanently lost touch with Reality.

As you can see, despite our sometimes complicated relationship, Reality is really out of sight in my book. I hope you enjoy reading it again and again until the pages are all dog-eared. It has been, after all, a pet project of mine.

IT IS MY SINCERE HOPE THAT MY PUBLICATION

QUICKLY BECOMES A SMASHING SUCCESS

KNOW WHAT I MEAN, JELLYBEAN?

It is strange how so many adults, who are always looking out for their children's best interest, go against their financial advisors' recommendations on Easter and encourage their children to put all of their eggs in one basket. I myself have diversified by providing lessons, hiring others to do the same, providing musical entertainment upon occasion...and now....writing and publishing.

I would encourage you to take a page out of my book, but I am a strong opponent of plagiarism.

I humbly ask that you consider referring others to me, whether they be local to Baltimore and be in need of in-home music instruction or looking for musical entertainment for an event, or to those in any location who would appreciate my publication and those yet to come...

Of course, it is completely your choice and I do not want to push you too much on the referrals, knowing that if you choose not to do so for any undisclosed reason, then it is simply none of my business.

IRONICALLY, THE ONLY WAY TO MAKE A JOYFUL SOUND

ON THE PIANO IS TO DEPRESS THE KEYS

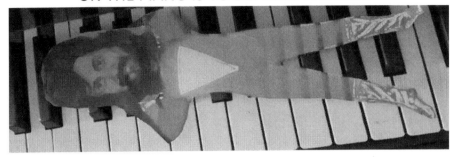

I HAVE A WHOLE OTHER WRITING STYLE AS WELL.

SERIOUSLY. NO JOKE(S).

My sense of humor and my propensity for using language for humorous purposes does not mean that I do not or cannot feel deeply or have a sense of reverence, or of the profound....having an upbeat attitude simply inspires me to uplift others and share a positive perspective. That can often be accomplished through humor.

But life can certainly provide experiences of great difficulty or of great joy and other deep or profound spiritual moments or of great passage in which humor has no place...

In my own personal life - such personal moments and events or my more serious contemplation of life itself and its ultimate meaning have inspired me to use my love of language to convey just that...

THE IMPORTANCE OF GIVING OF ONESELF

AS THE SEASONS PASS, ONE BY ONE, OUR AWARENESS MAY GROW AND COME TO RECOGNIZE THE GREATEST TRUTH THAT EXISTS- THAT WHAT WE GIVE TO OTHERS IS THE SOURCE OF OUR SACRED AND ETERNAL UNION WITH THE WORLD -- FOR IN THE OUTSTRETCHED HANDS OF BOTH THE GIVER AND RECEIVER LIES THAT SAME POTENTIAL THAT THEY MAY MEET- AND THEIR EXPERIENCES MAY INTERSECT - IF ONLY FOR WHAT SEEMS AN INSTANT...AND BOTH BECOME CHANGED FOREVER....

4/19/98

REFLECTION ON MY MOTHER'S UNTIMELY PASSING

(age 51)

IN NOVEMBER 1992

AS THE DAYS PASS, THE PAIN EASES; A PAIN BORN OF LOVE. WHILE GRIEF IS THE COST OF THE LOST OF A LOVED ONE, THE DEPTH OF SADNESS, WHILE PAINFUL, IS A MEASURE OF THAT LOVE. A FOUNTAIN OF SORROW SPRINGS FORTH ONLY FROM THAT WHICH HAS GIVEN MEANING. AS WE JOURNEY THROUGH THIS WORLD, THE EXPERIENCE OF GRIEF IS A GREAT TEACHER, FOR IT TEACHES THE TRUE VALUE OF JOYFUL TIMES. WE LEARN TO MORE GREATLY APPRECIATE THE ABSENCE OF PAIN, AND THROUGH OUR SUFFERING WE EARN STRENGTH...AND THROUGH THE EXPERIENCE, OUR EYES ARE OPENED TO THE BURDENS OF OTHERS.

AS I REFLECT UPON THE DAYS OF GREAT SORROW I
EXPERIENCED IN THE PASSING OF MY MOTHER, I WILL
ALWAYS REMEMBER THE LESSONS TAUGHT TO ME BY
NATURE. A GENTLE RAIN REFLECTED NOT ONLY MY TEARS
OF GRIEF, BUT THOSE OF MANY THROUGHOUT THE AGES
OF MANKIND. THE CHANGING OF THE LEAVES SWEETLY
WHISPERED OF CHANGE, AND THE CIRCLE OF BIRTH AND
DECAY....AND THE BIRDS, AS THEY SOARED ABOVE ME IN
MY MOMENTS OF DEEPEST PAIN, ABSORBED MY GREATEST
SORROWS, LIKE MESSENGERS FROM THE GREAT SPIRIT,
TRANSCENDENTAL IN THEIR GENTLE LOVING INSISTENCE
THAT FREEDOM LIES IN LETTING GO, THE CONTINUATION
OF THEIR FLIGHT SERVING TO SOW WITHIN ME THE SEEDS
OF THEIR COMPASSIONATELY IMPARTED WISDOM.

AND IT IS WITH A CLEANSED HEART, FILLED WITH
MEMORIES, THAT MY EYES SHALL CONTINUE TO BEHOLD
WITH GREAT WONDER, THE FREEDOM OF BIRDS AS THEY
SOAR THROUGH THE SKY, MIRRORING THE GRACE OF THE
GREAT SPIRIT, WHO GENTLY LIFTS UP OUR LOVED ONES,
WHO THEN TAKE TO FLIGHT AND IMPART WISDOM TO
THOSE IN NEED.

MARRIAGE PROPOSAL WRITING PRESENTED

TO MY FIANCE (to be), HARLENE

ON NEW YEAR'S EVE 1993/94

ONLY GRACE CAN BRING TOGETHER TWO SOULS WHO SOAR TO THE SONG OF LIFE.

WE ARE MADE OF THE TREES AND THE EARTH AND THE SUN AND THE MOON AND THE STARS AND THE WIND AND THE RIVERS.

THE TREES GIVE US OUR STRENGTH AND THE EARTH, OUR SUSTENANCE. THE SUN GIVES US OUR CLARITY, AND THE MOON OUR RHYTHMS. THE STARS GIVE US OUR DREAMS AND THE WIND AND RIVERS - OUR FORTUNE AND DIRECTION.

MAY OUR STRENGTH BUILD A STRONG FOUNDATION AND OUR SUSTENANCE HUMBLE US. MAY OUR CLARITY FOSTER WISDOM AND OUR RHYTHMS, BALANCE.

MAY OUR DREAMS RESOUND WITH INSPIRATION, OUR FORTUNE INSTILL GRATITUDE AND OUR DIRECTION EVER BE PAVED WITH CHALLENGE AND ADVENTURE.

WALKING ALONG THE SHORES WITH YOU - COMPOSED

ON 4/24/94 FOR MY (then) FIANCE

Harlene Andrea Davis (read by me at our wedding)

WHAT, YOU ASK, SAY I OF THE WOMAN WHO DANCES IN MY HEART? WHOSE EYES SPARKLE WITH THE RADIANCE OF A JOYOUS LIGHT WITHIN?

A TREASURE, SAY I, TO MY SOUL WAS WASHED UNTO THE SHORES OF THE SANDS UPON WHICH I WALK...

AN EMBRACE FROM HER SPARKS A FIRE DEEP WITHIN AND CONNECTS US WITH THE SOURCE OF ALL TRANSITORY EXPERIENCE.

INSTANTANEOUSLY, WE SURPASS HEIGHTS ONCE ASPIRED TO BY FRACTURED WINGS, WHICH LONGED FOR HEALING HANDS TO TOUCH, THUS MAKING EACH WHOLE.

SHOULD CASTLES BUILT TOGETHER IN THE SAND WITH LOVING HANDS BRING SADNESS BECAUSE THE TIDE WASHES THEM AWAY?

BETTER YET, MY LOVE, WILL WE HOLD FONDLY THE MEMORY OF OUR HUMBLE WORK.

...AND WE SHALL REJOICE IN THE ETERNAL PRESENT, WHICH LEAVES FREE OUR NOBLE HANDS FOR EVER WISER ENDEAVOR...

AS WE WALK ALONG THE SHORES OF LIFE, MAY WE REMAIN EVER AWARE THE WE ARE THE CHILDREN THAT PLAY IN THE SAND, FOR THEY ARE THE SONG IN OUR HEARTS...

...AND WE ARE THE SANDCASTLES, MOLDED BY PURPOSEFUL ACTION...

...AND WE ARE THE OCEAN...DANCING IN RHYTHM, YET EVER CONSTANT.

...AND WE ARE THE SEAGULLS, TRANSCENDENT - YET GRACEFULLY IN HARMONY WITH OUR SOURCE...

WHAT, YOU ASK, SAY I OF THE WOMAN WHO DANCES IN MY HEART?

MY COMPLETION, SAY I, LIES IN THE WELLSPRING OF HER LOVE.

A Very Special Remembrance of Charles "Turk" McGowan -

(My Paternal Grandfather) - 1995

(Or Perhaps a Remembrance of He Whom Endowed Me
with Musicality and Exuberance)

TO LIVE LIFE TO ITS ABSOLUTE FULLEST...TO BE COMPLETELY GENUINE AND DISMISS ALL PRETENSE, EVEN WHERE SOCIAL CONVENTION WOULD LEAD MOST TO THE POLITE SUPPRESSION OF THE TRUTH.

TO FEEL AND EXPRESS AN UTTER FASCINATION WITH LIFE ITSELF AND TO DEVELOP THE MIND TO THE GREATEST EXTENT THAT A LIFETIME PERMITS.

TO ACCEPT HUMAN NATURE AS IT IS, AND YET, IN SPITE OF IT, DEMONSTRATE GREATER GENEROSITY AND COMPASSION THAN MOST. TO SEIZE THE MOMENT AND TAKE FULL ADVANTAGE OF THE OPPORTUNITIES LIFE AFFORDS RATHER THAN, AS MANY DO, RESIGNING ONESELF TO THEIR MERE CONSIDERATION....

TO CULTIVATE THE CAPACITY FOR TRUE CONTENTMENT, AND, AT THE VERY DEEPEST LEVEL, SHARE THE MOST FUNDAMENTAL SECRET OF LIFE WITH HIS SPOUSE, FAMILY AND FRIENDS; THAT LIFE IS A BEAUTIFUL AND SACRED JOURNEY.

TURK TAUGHT US THAT LIFE IS, INDEED, A BEAUTIFUL AND SACRED JOURNEY, AND SHOWED US THAT ONCE WE REALIZE THIS---THAT THOSE THINGS OF GREATEST IMPORTANCE SHALL SHINE AS BRIGHTLY AS THE SUN.

THE LOVE THAT WE SHARED WITH THIS MOST REMARKABLE HUMAN BEING SHALL SHINE JUST AS BRIGHTLY WHENEVER WE FOLLOW THE EXAMPLE HE HAS GIVEN US.

WEDDING TOAST FOR MY DAD & HIS NEW WIFE, CLAUDIA

(C.J.) WRITTEN & READ ALOUD BY ME

AT THEIR WEDDING RECEPTION

ON OCTOBER 31, 1998

MAY YOUR HEARTS BE LIGHT AND YOUR JOY RUN

DEEP

MAY YOU REACH NEW HEIGHTS AS EACH OTHER

YOU KEEP

IN A LIFE OF ADVENTURE, WITH A LOVE THAT

STILL GROWS

LIKE A LONG WINDING ROAD OR A RIVER THAT

FLOWS

WHAT I'M TRYING TO TELL YOU, IF YOU HAVEN'T

BOTH GUESSED

IS WE ALL LOVE YOU DEARLY AND WISH YOU THE

BEST

Written in 1997 while we were trying to conceive a child.

In 2000 we adopted our son Stephen from Siberia

OUR PRECIOUS CHILD, YOU HAVE ENTERED THIS GREAT GARDEN IN ORDER TO CHANGE AND GROW...

MAY YOU ALWAYS REALIZE THAT ALL OF YOUR LIFE EXPERIENCE IS MEANT ONLY TO SERVE THIS GOAL...

USE THE TALENTS AND ABILITIES YOU HAVE BEEN GIVEN AND USE THEM TO SERVE OTHERS...

LOOK INSIDE AND YOU SHALL FIND THE ANSWERS WHICH YOU SEEK...

MAY YOU FIND STRENGTH IN DIFFICULT TIMES... THEY WILL DEEPEN YOU TO THE JOY OF GREATER EXPERIENCES THAT AWAIT YOU...

THEN, EVEN WHEN WE HAVE SAILED OUT OF SIGHT, YOU WILL NOT ONLY REMEMBER US, BUT YOU WILL SEE US IN ALL OF THE BEAUTY THAT SURROUNDS YOU...AND AS YOU SAIL YOUR BOAT THROUGH THIS LIFE YOU WILL REMAIN EVER-CONNECTED TO THE GREAT CIRCLE OF LIFE IN WHICH WE EMBRACE YOU FOREVER...

AUTHOR SCOTT PATRICK Mc GOWAN WITH HIS WIFE,
HARLENE & THEIR SON, STEPHEN – adopted in 2000 from

Siberia.

PHOTO IS FROM A FRONT PAGE ARTICLE PUBLISHED ABOUT
THEIR BUSINESS IN THE BALTIMORE'S JEFFERSONIAN (2002)

DEDICATION TO HARLENE

Not only to me, but to everyone you met. You are so beautiful. The agreement is unanimous, yet I think strangely you hardly knew. You were a champion of everyone's well-being, wanting everyone to know how important they were in their own right. Striving to make sure all knew this. Striving always and only to uplift all you encountered. To understand them, to help them, yes and to love them, often nearly immediately.

How lucky that besides all of that, I, in addition got to be your best friend, lover, and business partner. Together we became adoptive parents and brought our precious Stephen home from a Siberian orphanage and gave him a better life here. It seems you left just as we reached a new level of mutual understanding from lessons learned, some of them painful for both of us.

You turned your personal wounds into unconditional gifts to others and were blossoming into a woman who finally was beginning to acknowledge her own beauty, to bravely heal those wounds and claim what should have been yours as a birthright.

Each piano student you ever took on was like a fragile and unique gem to you. You saw what the world could be and planted only the best of seeds everywhere you went, thinking nothing of how much conscious care you took, without fail, in every encounter to ensure that you brightened everyone's journey and even gave unexpected and insightful new, important, perhaps even life-changing self-understanding to friends and virtual strangers alike. Something you implicitly found as an unquestioned principle. It should be, and if only it weren't so lacking as an unspoken social contract, what a beautiful world this would be.

But know this: the pain I feel in the wake of your sudden departure from this world has been met with a level of support so rare, that surely all know the beauty of your soul was also so rare that in turn my loss is all the greater as well as theirs.

What a precious gem have you been in this world. May your soul fly free knowing, as Tony wrote, "Promise we all pull together to help your Main Man, Scott." I'd say around 100 or more people stepping through the door since I shockingly found that you were no longer with us over just a few day period proves you can count on that promise.

I know we always loved the quote in What Dreams May Come: "Sometimes When You Lose You Win." I've had a handful of important intuitions in my life, though not nearly as many as you. I always thought that quote would have an important meaning in my life at some point the first time we watched it together. I am now certain that it relates to losing you and someday I will understand that. A future event or circumstance that is intertwined somehow with your passing that will be a gift to me...

I had a dream a few days before your passing that unmistakably told me you would be leaving. As unmistakably as the accidental snapping and falling off of my mother's memorial bracelet from my wrist only days after arriving home with our beautiful son Stephen, surely dreaming of a silver bracelet, yet again snapping off of my wrist meant that a huge passage in my life was arriving shortly.

Surely somehow all is in Divine Order. How else would the universe be able to tell me what was coming shortly? Harlene you are so incredibly loved by so many, and I too am discovering that I am loved even more than I knew as well. I love you Harlene. I love you all...

FOREVER IN MY HEART

Made in the USA
Columbia, SC
05 May 2018